Growing up in HINDPOOL

Barrow-in-Furness

An illustrated local history by

Stan Henderson

First published in 2019 by Stan Henderson

© Copyright Stan Henderson
www.retro-books.co.uk

ISBN: 978-1-9160217-4-7

Second Edition 2024

Book & Cover Design by Russell Holden

www.pixeltweakspublications.com

A Catalogue record for this book is available from the British Library.

Printed by Ingram

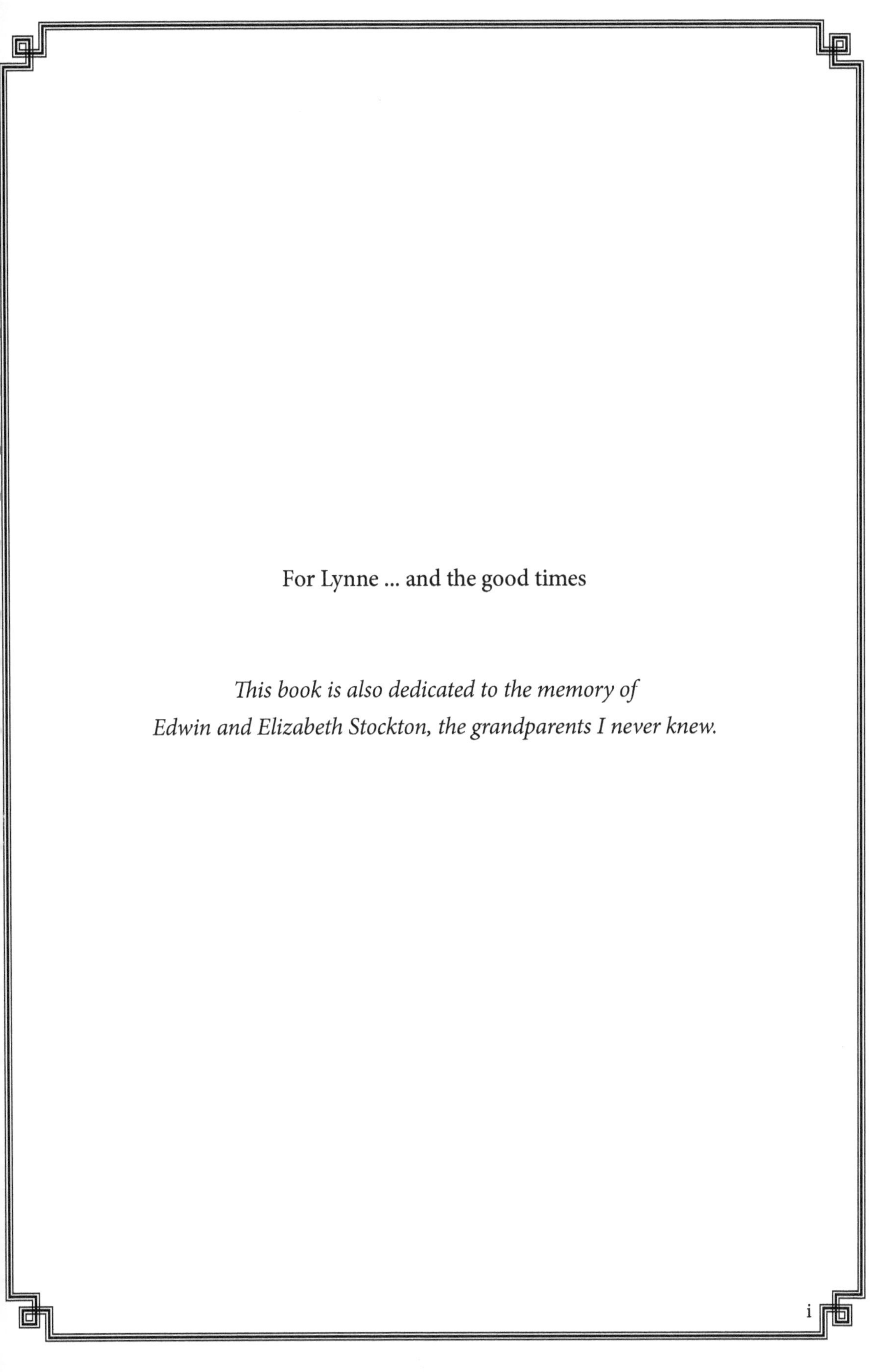

For Lynne ... and the good times

This book is also dedicated to the memory of
Edwin and Elizabeth Stockton, the grandparents I never knew.

Hindpool

Hindpool was the location of the once mighty Haematite Steel Company (incorporated in 1864) which, in two separate centuries, was at the forefront of steelmaking technology.

The works were, originally, erected to stand or fall by the manufacturing of steel ingots by the new Bessemer process and the rolling of said ingots into rails, on a scale hitherto never before contemplated. It was a bold experiment.

Many years later, during the 1950s, the aforementioned ingots would be tossed onto the proverbial scrap heap when Barrow works developed a high-speed process for the continuous casting of steel billets and slabs. This new process consigned several steps of orthodox steelmaking to the history books.

Although not conceived in Barrow, the continuous casting of steel, in twenty years, had not advanced beyond the experimental stage. What Barrow achieved - during six years of intense development work, when the alchemy was lighted upon - was to progress the concept into a commercially viable process; again making history.

Contents

Acknowledgements

This book was made possible because of the invaluable input from many sources – family and friends – too numerous to list here although special thanks are extended to John Baker; Albert Brennan; Roger Brill-Edwards; John Sadler also Jack and Alan Stockton and John Young. The ground work undertaken by students James Melville; Ray Hewson; Bryn Trescatheric and Alice Leach have proved invaluable, giving me a foundation upon which to build my Hindpool story.

A facility I have always used, and I hope the reader will indulge me here, has been to liken people – usually those who have had some authority over me – to celebrities. I do this where I have been unable to source a photograph of the person being discussed. In my view it is a light-hearted way of getting around a problem whilst adding, perhaps, a touch of humour to the narrative.

Thanks are also due to two colleagues who have been with me across four books now; these are Ken Royall for his expert photographic input, advice and encouragement. Also local artist Geoffrey Berry, of Walney Island, who was prepared to suspend work on his own projects in favour of mine.

Stan Henderson, Author

Geoffrey Berry, artist

Ken Royall, Photographer

I also need to offer thanks to Susan Benson of Cumbria Archives and Local Studies Centre (Barrow) for kindly sourcing various records and images for inclusion. Also her colleagues Selena Kendall and Paul Moore, whose help is also appreciated and to Russell Holden of Pixel Tweaks for producing this book.

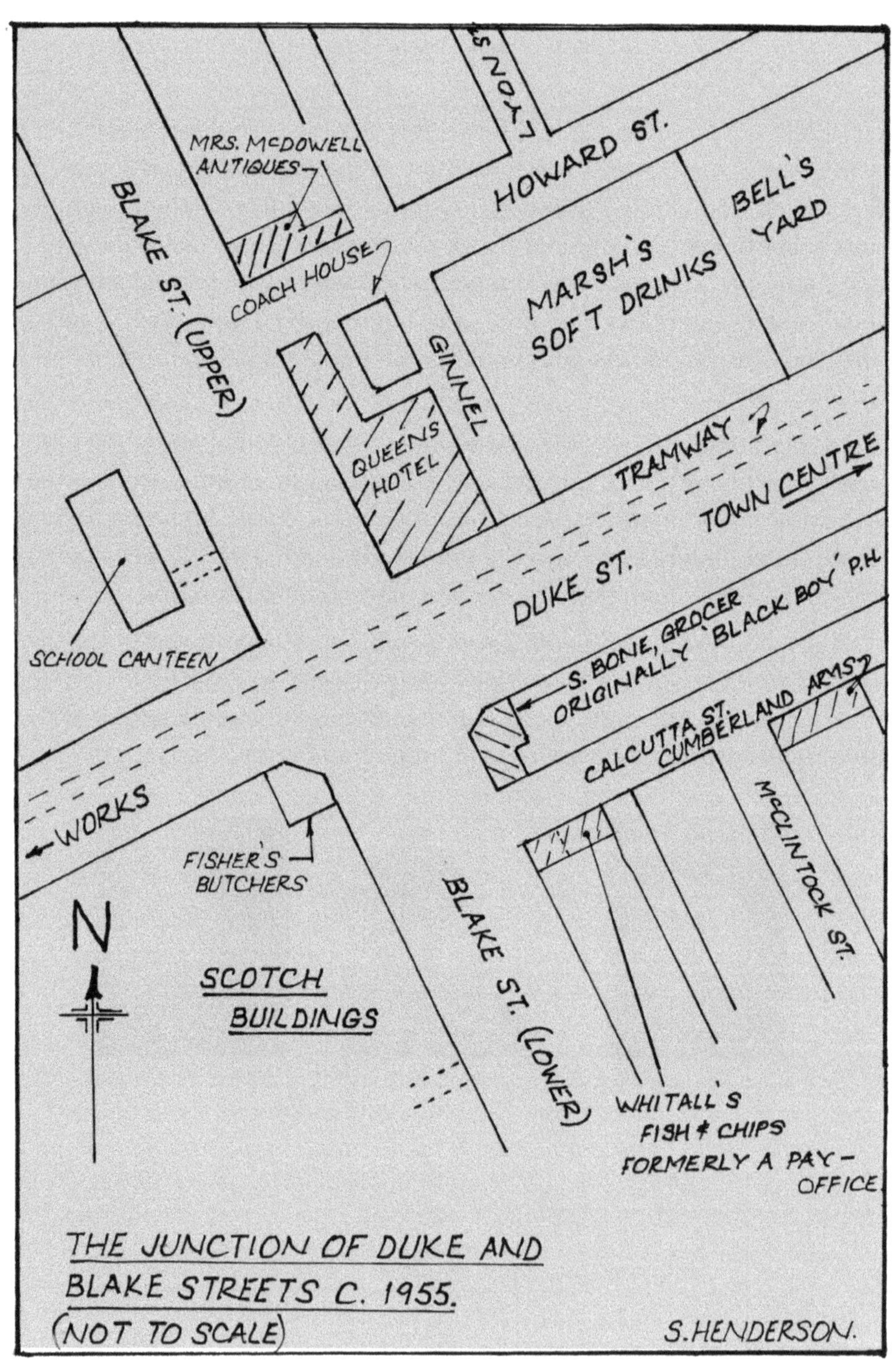

Sketch depicting the junction of Duke Street and Blake Street around 1955; for many years the tramway to/from the Steelworks terminus was the defining boundary between Upper and Lower Hindpool. From the early-1930s, motor buses began to replace the trams.

Introduction

This is a story about friends, families, characters and growing up in Barrow-in-Furness. As with a previous book – *A Piper's Tale* - it has been culled, chiefly, from family history and in some ways could be regarded as a prequel to the aforementioned title. The setting for the narrative is Hindpool, which was originally in the parish of Dalton-in-Furness. *"Hynepulle"*, as it was known to the monks of Furness, was first mentioned in the Dalton *court rolls* of 1537. The district, during my recall, was divided into Upper and Lower. This was not because of any class-distinction aspect. Hindpool is bisected by the main thoroughfare, Duke Street, which effectively splits it in two. Moreover, during the early days of Barrow's development, Lower Hindpool was populated by, mainly, migrant workers – which included my ancestors - the Stocktons. This book is an attempt to recount at least part of the history.

The first part of the story and as told in chapter one, covers the coming to the town of my great-great grandparents – immigrants from Shropshire – to work on the Hindpool blast furnaces. There is also a glimpse at the social conditions of the time. This part of the book is, obviously, 'before living memory' and has been researched from the local records of the Cumbria Archive and Local Studies Centre (Barrow). Although sources are listed after each chapter, to assist the historic researcher, this book is aimed more at the general reader.

The second part – from chapter three - is about life in, mainly, post-war Hindpool including school days when some teachers took the meaning of *in loco parentis* too literally.

Hindpool, in the years following the war, was an exciting place for a boy to grow up. Places in which to play and explore – totally unsafe in hindsight – abounded. Two of my favourite sites were the ruins of the *Barrow & Calcutta Jute Works*, which was next to Lakeland Laundries, also the clay quarry of the *Furness Brick & Tile Company*, which was also the location of the derelict *Whinsfield* mansion. Additionally, the official play area at *Piggy Lane* was enjoyed by all Hindpool children – both boys and girls.

There was also, in the district, a core of *mysterious* older people, hermit-types who kept to themselves but I would wager all had interesting tales to tell. One example I encountered was Owen, who lived alone on Walney Road. He worked at the Slag Reduction Works. Owen had the appearance of a *vagrant* and he never spoke to anyone. Following his death, dozens of unopened wage packets were found under his bed. Moreover, his house contained many *antiques* and items of *curio*, obviously left by his parents, the identity of whom are lost in time. Another character, who lived at the top of Franklin Street and on the corner of Calcutta Street opposite the shop, was only ever known to us as *Popeye*. Whenever you saw him he would be pushing a wheel barrow that had two cast iron wheels. It is said that he retained the first shilling he was given.

More importantly, there was this *vestigial feel* that Hindpool, in earlier times, had had this awesome dynamic and we were now living in the wake of its former glory. Of necessity, I have stretched the boundaries of the district so as to include such as Fell Street; Ferry Beach; Osborne Street; Holker Street School and Barrow AFC. In writing my story I have tried to be frank, setting events and people down as I saw and experienced them at the time. Some may take the view that I have been too frank – but at least I believe I have been honest. Digressions, factoids and other items incidental to the main narrative are set in italics. This second edition includes some additional information.

All opinions expressed are entirely my own, for which, as well as all errors, I take full responsibility.

It is hoped you enjoy the read.   *S. Henderson, 2018 /2024*

Chapter One

Coming To Barrow

The following is an unedited transcript of some of the last words spoken by my uncle, Sydney Stockton, when in St Mary's Hospice, Ulverston, during October, 2008:-

"I was born in 'rooms' in Newport Street, Barrow in 1923. The family lived in rooms in those days because of the housing shortage and the slump after the Great War. My father, Edwin Stockton, lived at 91 Holker Street, and at the age of 17 took it into his head to sign-up and so went to do the honours, (1914).

'How old are you?' asked the recruiting sergeant. 'Seventeen', replied Edwin. The sergeant told him to take a turn around the block and come back. This he did and was asked the same question. 'Eighteen', replied dad. He was given the King's Shilling and signed-up.

Edwin was shot in his right thigh. Upon recuperating he was sent to France.

After the end of the War he was seen (on film), marching along in a parade immediately behind a pipe band. His two sisters, Ann and Alice, when in the Gaiety cinema stood up and shouted, 'There's our Teddy'.

Seven years out of work was the reward for the wartime slog during which time he met my mother, Mary Elizabeth Bowman. They wed and took rooms in Newport Street [with the Lovelly family]. They later moved to Beech Street (Cemetery Cottages), with friends of the people they had lived with at Newport Street.

Families grow and my sister Joan was born, unfortunately with one of her hips out of place. We next moved to Lime Street with mother's brother George Bowman (Uncle George). George had lost a finger due to a gunshot wound. He had a hut at Sandscale Haws, also known as Lowsy Point – people referred to them as the Black Huts. He also owned a small, open boat – which we tarred twice per year in an effort to keep it water-tight.

Another brother, Frank, was born in 1929 and he was born with both of his hips displaced. So with four children to keep a house of their own was needed. One was found courtesy of Marsh's Aerated Water. Aunt Alice had married Walter Marsh. The house they were offered was 35 Back Dalton Road, (later Fell Street). The new home came with the proviso that they look after father's mother [our Nan], and this was agreed. A little later brother Jack was born and this time everything was intact. Soon after dad secured a job in Vickers as a slinger in the Gun Shop. He did one week on day shift and one week on nights. Edwin had two brothers, Frank and John. Frank was the eldest. I never knew him as he went off to Canada under the immigration scheme along with quite a few others at the time. I believe that he later returned to Barrow where he died from Polio".

Syd passed away on 18th October, 2008.

When starting to write this book, the foregoing was all that I knew of the Stockton – Bowman side of the family.

The Stocktons, along with thousands of others during the second half of the 19th century, came to Barrow to find work and to, hopefully, secure some kind of a future. The reason for the mass migration into the town could be summarised into just one word – **_iron!_**

Although iron ore had been mined and worked in the district from *antiquity,* it was not until 1853, when the Park deposits were found (*the largest in British history up to that time*) that Barrow began to be wrenched from its rural obscurity.

Founding father, James Ramsden, had identified the location for an iron smelting works but the land, which bordered the Barrow foreshore, was not owned by the town's benefactor - the Earl of Burlington. It was owned by the Cranke family of Urswick and Ulverston. John Cranke, a solicitor, was a shareholder in the fledgling *Furness Railway Company*. The land in question, around 160-acres, was known as the Hindpool Estate and it came up for sale in 1854 for the sum of £7000. The *Furness Railway Company* made the purchase and then, for 'a modest rent' leased it to Messrs Schneider and Hannay – who had previously been interested in mining in the area – for the erection of blast furnaces.

Going into production in October 1859, these early furnaces were only 45-feet high, being increased to 62-feet in 1871[2]. They were open-topped, allowing the hot gases* generated by the smelting process to escape to atmosphere. *These hot gases would have, intermittently, flashed to flame thereby being quite a spectacle across the night sky.*

Adam Stockton originated from a small village in *Salop Wem (an old name for Shropshire)*, called *Norton-in-Hales*, about 4-miles from Stoke-on-Trent. He is listed in the 1861 Census as being an agricultural labourer with six children. The Stocktons were part of the ongoing trend whereby folk were moving from the agrarian and into the industrial, from the rural to the urban. Moreover, it's possible their move was also because of the agricultural *slump* precipitated by developments in America during the 1870s. They moved to Dudley, where they stayed for a while, and then in 1876 came to Barrow, where Adam secured employment with what had become the *Barrow Haematite Steel Company*. He would have started, as most unskilled workers did in those days, as a labourer or, more specifically, a *pig lifter or a barrow wheeler.*

The furnaces at that time were connected along their tops with a high-level platform. This platform was used to convey the charge – via

---

* Some books about the iron industry refer, erroneously, to the hot gases as waste gases. There was no waste from a bf, only by-products. Everything produced had a commercial value.

The Hindpool bf's c. 1899, the Furness Railway main line can be seen with a wagon being loaded with cast iron pigs; this image also shows the high-level platforms that were used by the barrow wheelers, the furnaces at this time were 62-feet high. The photo was taken from the wrought iron foot-bridge that connected the two sections of the works.
Courtesy of Cumbria Archives and Local Studies Centre, Barrow.

wheelbarrows - from the hoists to each furnace. It was a strenuous and sometimes risky occupation. Four years later the job was to prove too risky for 46-year old Bill Hartley of Back Hartington Street[†].

It was one day in March, 1880 that the charging gang at No 2 hoist had finished loading their carriage with coke. This was to be hauled up the inclined plane and then barrowed to No 5 blast furnace. The hoist engine driver, Bill Woodward was given the signal and the four barrow-wheelers mounted the loaded car as it began its ascent. About halfway up they noticed their speed was faster than normal and, as they weren't slowing as they approached the top, prepared to jump clear. At the top all of the four men made a spring to gain the upper platform but William Hartley, father of five, never managed the leap and, as one of the winding ropes had broken, was now on a white-knuckle ride back down to the charging depot. The wrought-iron carriage smashed into the stops at the bottom flinging Hartley violently forwards trap-

† Back Hartington Street: being either Keyes St (west) or, Wordsworth Street (east)

ping him between some barrows. He was taken to hospital where it was found that his skull was fractured, his jaw broken and his leg was also smashed. He died the next day from 'severe concussion'.

The *Barrow Herald* of 23rd March carried a report of the inquest which concluded that, whilst the incident was very tragic, there was an overall low number of fatal accidents at the Barrow works which, at the time employed over three thousand men. The accident was deemed statistically insignificant. *[It would not be until just after the First World War, when the furnaces were remodelled, that mechanised charging was introduced].*

The Stocktons found accommodation in Lower Hindpool. Adam and his wife, Ann, at 22 McClintock Street, his eldest son Edward and his family moved into a house at 34 Clive Street[3]. A few years later Adam's daughter, Clara, took a job at the *Jute Works*. The Stockton's mid-terrace house on McClintock Street was adjacent to a butcher's premises which is recorded as having small slaughterhouse facilities in the yard to the rear. From my recollection of these properties 'small' was the operative word and I would have wagered that nothing larger than poultry was ever processed there. Directly opposite 22 had been *The Boat* beer house but this had closed down in 1866.

The austerities of life in Victorian Hindpool cannot be overstated. For the newly-arrived Stocktons it is not known whether they enjoyed a house to themselves or, as with most families, had to share. It had been reported that in some households beds were never cold. As one person arose for the day shift, someone coming off night-shift would immediately slink into his bed[1]. Probably without first bathing, or even washing. Houses were lit by gas *(down-stairs only)*, candles being used to 'light you to bed'. *When at Infants school in the mid-fifties, I can remember visiting school friends' homes in Clive Street* where gas lighting was still in use (Aird's at No 62 was one example). Additionally, *Zachariah Charnley's newsagents at 40 Lower Anson Street still had gas lighting into the Fifties. Their living quarters were created by a large bed sheet, which hung from curtain wire, draped across the retail area, which effectively split the shop area in half.*

The relaxation needs of working people were fulfilled outside of the home in these times. *(The Sony PlayStation was still, about, 150 years in the future).* For cultural purposes the *Theatre Royal* on Albert Street, built in 1864, featured Shakespearian productions, while the *Alexandra Music Hall* in Forshaw Street – Barrow's first music hall and built in 1866 – catered for 'lighter' tastes. Additionally, the *Alhambra Palace*, a music hall which opened on New Year's Day in 1872 on Cavendish Street, had a seating capacity of almost 2000. *All this without an Arts Council grant!* Here, many workpeople were able to find their Saturday night relaxation. For those not so inclined, there were the local beer houses of which Lower Hindpool boasted as many as 17 during one period. Wherever intoxicating liquor was being consumed there would always be characters [as well as drunkenness]. *Later, during the post-WWII years, things were no different, as the reader will discover upon reaching Chapter Seven.* Hindpool had always had its share of *rum* characters. One incident in particular, described as a right *rum do*, occurred prior to the Stockton's arrival in the town. It took place at the *Cumberland Arms.*

The *Cumberland* was a purpose-built, end of terrace beer house which stood at the corner of McClintock Street and Back Duke Street (later Calcutta Street). Its licensee, John Vanes was of good character with a reputation for honesty. His only appearance in court was in September, 1866 to testify to a rather peculiar practical joke perpetrated at the Inn. Local tailor, John Burton was on his way to deliver

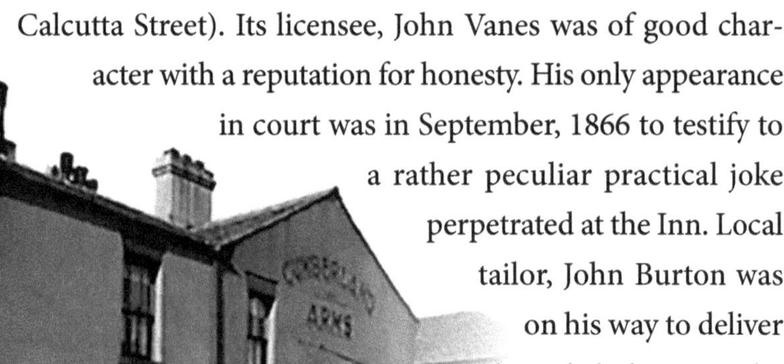

The Cumberland Arms on Calcutta Street (scene of a very peculiar practical joke). This was the only Hindpool public house I had never set foot in – possibly because I would have found it too claustrophobic. The licensee during the 1960s was Norman Squire, a keen angler. I recall that he would regularly charter a boat we had at the time for his fishing trips into Morecambe Bay.

a pair of trousers to a client when he decided to stop off at the *Cumberland* for a bite to eat.

He recalled ordering two pennyworth of bread and cheese and a glass of ale before his mind went a complete blank. It was at this point that Mr Burton felt he had been drugged with chloroform. His next memory was of being approached by a stranger, in Duke Street, who was concerned about his appearance. The stranger, a woman, pointed out to him that his face had been blackened with boot polish, his hat had been cut into the shape of a crown and pieces of paper, upon which amusing slogans had been written, had been pinned to his jacket. He then noticed three men, who were standing in the doorway of the *Ambrose Hotel* on Duke Street, pointing at him and laughing. Angered by this Burton approached the men and demanded they explain why they made him look such a fool? Burton then alleged the men dragged him into a room in the Ambrose pushing and pulling him around, during which his trousers and jacket became torn beyond repair.

Later, when in court, roars of laughter boomed out from the gallery as Burton provided his testimony and reason for bringing the three men before the magistrates. The laughter increased more during the cross-examination that followed. It was put to the tailor, on several occasions that he may have been drunk. He refused to accept this, stating that such a notion was 'utter nonsense'. The poor fellow remained convinced that he had been drugged with chloroform – this being the only explanation. John Vanes was called as witness and questioned as to how such an event could occur inside his Inn without his notice? Vanes insisted that nothing of the sort happened on the day in question. Vanes also confirmed that Burton presented as being very excitable when he came into the pub. Asked by the Bench if he thought Burton to be drunk, he stated that he was clearly not drunk, just acting oddly. The magistrates chose to dismiss the case based on Vane's testimony. They never questioned the three men and so the mystery remained unsolved![6].

When considering the subject of *leisure* in these times two things must be borne in mind. Firstly, the time factor. Employees of the blast furnace plant could be working twelve-hour shifts with Saturday still a working day. Secondly, the labour by which the majority made a living was heavy and fatiguing. And although Sunday was a day of rest for most, few would have had the energy to run marathons! For those so inclined and with the absence of a public park, the grounds of Furness Abbey or even Walney Island were good walking territory[1]. Additionally, attendance at local sporting events provided an alternative outlet for many as Furness had a healthy and diverse sporting scene. Track and Field events including wrestling were popular and folk could attend gatherings at Walney, also at Dalton and Ulverston.

Despite the hardship it would be fair to say that the homes of iron and steelworkers [as with their beds] were never really cold. The works, at the time, were consuming almost half a million tons of coal per year. This was brought from the work's collieries in wagons of the *Furness Railway Company*[1]. There was low-sulphur coal for gas production; coking- coal for the smelting processes; steam-coal to power the plant and locomotives and coal for the turbo-generators. The Hindpool works were awash with the stuff. As a consequence, workers were going home with their bait tins and pockets full – some even had 'poacher's pockets' sewn into their overcoats. At one point the problem became so bad that management insisted that, once unloaded from the wagons (at the northern-end of the works in an area

Typical Tommy Tin (Bait Box) and Tea & Sugar container. These were useful for taking things into (and out of) the works. Susan Blake, 1980.

known as *Skull Island*), a great wall of coal be constructed, which was then white-washed[5]. The reasoning being was that anyone helping themselves would leave a *black hole* in the wall. Whether the tactic was successful or not is not recorded. As well as coal, wood for kindling was also taken by workers. *During my short time there I found that Harold McCracken, a man on permanent secondment from the Wigan Wagon Co., had a sideline going whereby pieces of 6 x 2 timber from old railway wagons were cut up so as to neatly fit into the mens' tommy tins. These blocks of timber, for some unexplained reason, were referred to as cock-wood. In exchange for his fire-wood, Harold would receive such as eggs, fresh fish, rabbits and sweets – fine examples of bartering.*

After three years at Hindpool, Adam moved his family to Askam-in-Furness taking his newly acquired skills to the ironworks there. Investors *Wakefield, Mackinnon & Company,* in 1865, had arranged for an iron smelting works – the *Furness Iron Co* - at a location to the south of the townlet in an area known as *The Lots**. Four blast furnaces had been erected on the 50-acre site, which employed about 300-men. Smelting commenced in August 1867 using, mainly, imported skill[4] . *The works were defined by the disproportionately tall boiler house* chimney, which was 325-feet high, *(dem 1930).*

High on a Hill, Ireleth Cemetery overlooking the Duddon Estuary and Black Combe. 'A ram's head butting at the bright turf and brackeny brine, gathers its own wool, plucks shadow out of shine'. Final resting place of Adam Stockton (1816 – 1883), with acknowledgements to Norman Nicholson. *Photo S. Henderson, 2018.*

The Stocktons moved into a house at Steel Street then later, Sharp Street. Within the first year at Askam, Adam's chronic lung condition** worsened to the point where he could no longer work [*He had worked for*

* Lots: aka 'Land of goose shit and feathers' per seldom seen map No 2 Furness peninsula

some time in a colliery prior to coming to Barrow and this may have been a factor]. He died in 1883 aged 67 from *Broncho-pneumonia* - and was interred at Ireleth Cemetery.

Following his father's death, Edward continued to work as a *blast furnace keeper.* Living at 91 Holker St, previously at 12, 14 Osborne Street‡ - Grandad Edwin was born at number 12 in 1896.

It is not known how the Stocktons fared a few years later when the Hindpool works closed down causing great distress for local folk. Had it not been for the soup kitchens run by St James's church, would many have starved to death? One day, a reporter from the *Barrow Herald* had accompanied the curate on one of his daily visits to the homes of the unemployed. To his horror, he discovered homes without any furniture, floor coverings and curtains. Everything had been sold or pawned. Everywhere he went he saw cold and starving families. The Council and the Church rallied support from local businesses and suppliers and donations of the ingredients necessary for soup making began to come in. The Council arranged for two wooden huts to be built in the rear yard of the school next to the church wall. One hut had three gas boilers installed. *[I recall seeing these huts, and the gas boilers, when I first attended St James' in, about, 1953].* In one boiler porridge was made, which was available from 7.30am, soup was made in the others.

In her book – *Working Class Barrow and Lancaster, 1896 to 1930* – Elizabeth Roberts alleges that over a period of twenty months, the Hindpool Soup Kitchen was estimated to have fed two million people.

** Lung conditions such as bronchitis and pneumonia were common among iron and steelworkers of the 19th century; per reference 1

‡ Osborne Street: the Stocktons, together with a family called Morgan, had connections with all three addresses in the street.

The Ironworks at Askam-in-Furness (originally the Furness Iron Company then later the Askam & Mouzell Iron Company, it officially closed in 1907 but was later reopened to support the war effort (1914-18), using Spanish ores. *Sankey Ref: 2386*

Sources & Notes to Chapter One.

1 *Furness and the Industrial Revolution*: J. D. Marshall, 1958

2 *Barrow Steel – A Brief History & Survey of Productions*: Ed J. Burrow & Co Ltd; 1937

3 1881 also 1891 Census for England.

4 *Furness and Cartmel Mannex Directory*, 1882.

5 Personal communication with Alan Stockton and ex-steelworker, Bill Pearson.

6 With acknowledgements to and paraphrased from *The Beer Houses of Barrow-in-Furness*: Alan Wilkinson, 2017.

Chapter Two

1920s and 30s

I never knew my grandparents Edwin Stockton and Mary Elizabeth (Lizzie) Bowman. They had both died long before I was born. Edwin was born in Osborne Street, Mary Elizabeth in Emlyn Street, Barrow. They had met each other through George (Barney) Bowman, who was Lizzie's brother. The Bowmans lived in the Cemetery Cottages. Edwin and Barney had served together in France during the Great War. After the war Barney had managed to get himself back into the steelworks and into a well-paid job. No such luck for Edwin, who endured many years of unemployment during the dark ages of the early 1920s. [*The Barrow & District Year Book called 1921 a 'black year'*].

Together with their four children, Sydney George; Joan; John (Jack) and Frank, they moved from Lime Street and into 35 Fell Street sometime during 1931. Number 35 was situated next to the end of the terrace at it's junction with Cavendish Street. The end property, at the time, being occupied by a bill posting company who stored such as ladders and buckets there. Next door in the other direction was the Johns family (Alice and William at 37). These people would turn out to be good friends to the family in the coming years. In the middle of the terrace was a Thompson's off-licence, this was run, during the 1930's by a family called Maguire. The shop stood out from the rest of the houses having an external sandstone wall, it was also one story higher. The Fell Street house (35), was owned and had previously been occupied by Edwin's sister, Alice, and her husband Walter Marsh. [Walter's family later owned the mineral water factory on Duke Street]. The house was provided, rent-free, in return for continuing to accommodate Edwin's mother, Eliza.

Eventually, Edwin managed to get a job as a slinger in the Gun Shop at Vickers. His shift pattern comprised a week of days and then a week on night shift, but despite now being in full-time employment he struggled to provide for his family. Edwin was a quiet sort of a man who rarely frequented the pub – unless, on occasion, he was with Barney, when they would go into Barney's local, the *Bankfield* at North Scale on Walney Island, enjoying a glass of ale and smoking the occasional Woodbine. Uncle Jack told me that Edwin enjoyed listening to Gracie Fields but couldn't afford to buy a radio. "He would listen to the next door neighbour's set by placing his [good] ear up to the dividing wall between the two houses and woe betide us if we made a noise while Gracie was singing". During the early 1930s, Vickers did not provide holiday pay for the annual summer holidays (effectively a *lock-out*), which caused hardship for many families. The Stocktons, therefore, would spend this time at Lowsy Point, staying in Barney Bowman's cabin and living off the land. (There was an abundance of chewit eggs at Sandscale Haws and the fishing was good). Such was the family's diet for their 'holiday'.

Jack Stockton explained to me that, in order to get to the black huts at Lowsy Point, they would first walk from Fell Street to the Ormsgill Hotel. From there Edwin would make four trips to the railway crossing near to Hayton's farm. "Each trip would see one of us riding on the cross-bar of dad's bike", he said. "On one occasion Uncle George took us to see Mr Tatham, a Hermit[§], who lived in a dug-out deep into the sand dunes".

Mother told us countless times of their childhood days in 1930s Barrow. "Urban life during the 1930s consisted of school [*Thwaite Street Juniors*] and then at weekends, we would visit either the Electric cinema, aka the

§ The Hermit, Mr Tatham, was the brother-in-law of Mrs Tatham who is in the photo on p15.

Bug Hut, (this was at the end of our street with the main entrance on Buccleuch Street) or the Regal on Forshaw Street. It would all depend on what was showing. Occasionally we would attend the Gaiety on Abbey Road. We weren't given pocket money, just the 1d admission to the pictures", she said. *"We earned pocket money by running errands for neighbours, I would then treat myself to a portion of chips and scratchings from the chip shop that years later became the Copper Kettle, on Buccleuch Street"*, said Uncle Jack. At the Regal during one particular week in January 1936, Al Jolson was singing about '*This Hurley-burley world of radio and steam*'[4], while over at the Gaiety, Bing Crosby crooned '*Two for To-night*' to co-star Joan Bennett. Our parents were happy for us to be at the cinema, as they knew where we were.

On Sundays dad always made breakfast, usually bacon and eggs and we would get half an egg each. Sometimes we had gulls eggs which Uncle George would bring. After our *feast*, weather permitting, we would go out for a walk. Nearly all of our *leisure* in these times comprised of 'going for a walk'. Walking was free, good for us and filled in time. Occasionally dad would take himself off to Sowerby Wood on his bike to pick wild flowers, sometimes dandelions from which he made wine. More often than not he would don his best suit and bowler hat then take the four of us to Furness Abbey.

The Electric Theatre (the Lec or Bug Hut) on Buccleuch Street. The Town's first purpose-built picture house and second home to the Stockton children through the 1930s. Courtesy of The Mail, 1957.

Cinema options in 1936. Facsimile of poster – Barrow Amusement Guide, week commencing 13 January, 1936

On the way home, walking along Abbey Road, we would call in on the Marshes, Aunt Alice and Uncle Walter, at *The Willows*, East Mount. Here we would be treated to one small bottle of mineral – either Orangeade or Sass – to be shared between the four of us! We were underwhelmed by their generosity.

For Sunday tea we would have bread and jam and then later we listened to Sydney practising his singing, occasionally helping with the descant. Syd was a member of St Mark's choir. After this it would be bed, 6pm in the winter and 8pm in summer. Dad was very strict in this regard. Uncle Jack recalled, years later. *"Many a time while in bed we could hear friends playing outside in the street. We thought that dad was tough on us at times"*.

Ad for Marsh's Mineral Water Factory. 'The House that Quality built' *Barrow & District Year Book, 1950.*

Tea Party on the beach: Residents of Fell Street and Cavendish Street on the shore at Sandy Gap, Walney in 1936. Left to right: Alice Marsh; Dorothy Bond; Frank Stockton (pouring tea); Jack Stockton; Mrs Waters; Billy Waters; Mary Elizabeth Stockton; Mrs Tatham (pouring tea); Tommy Bond (school cap) and Mrs Bond. *Stockton family photo.*

UNABLE TO HEAR ENGINE WHISTLE

BARROW MAN KILLED BY EXCURSION TRAIN

HEARING IMPAIRED BY COLD

A verdict of "Accidental Death" was returned at an inquest at Barrow Police Buildings this afternoon into the circumstances attending the death of Edwin Stockton, 40, a slinger, of 35, Fell-street, Barrow.

The Coroner for Furness, Mr. F. W. Poole, sat with a jury of which Mr. S. Hunt was foreman.

Evidence of identification was given by George Bowman, labourer, 43, of Lime-street, Barrow, deceased's brother-in-law.

Bowman later stated that Stockton had had a cold for the past two or three weeks, and had consequently been a "little hard in hearing."

William Jones, of 37, Fell-street, an unemployed cauker, said that he last saw deceased at about 8 p.m. on Sunday, when the latter told him he was going to Sowerby Woods to gather wild flowers.

The finding of the body, from which the legs had been severed at the waist, followed a report by the driver of the first train from Barrow to Askam on Monday of an object on the line near Sandscale crossing.

A bunch of flowers was found near the body.

Investigation at Manchester showed splashes of blood and a piece of flesh near the buffers on the locomotive which drew the 8.5 p.m. train from Workington on Sunday. The train was an excursion to Oldham which passed Sandscale crossing at about 10.12 p.m.

The driver of the train, John Brocklebank, of 24, Queen-street, Workington, said he sounded his whistle when about 300 yards from the crossing.

Summing-up the coroner said he had no doubt that deceased died from injuries accidentally received when he was knocked down by the train. Had his hearing been normal he might have heard the engine whistle and have escaped.

In summer and if the weather was particularly good, several families from the neighbourhood would set off to walk to Walney, especially as the toll had been lifted on the recently renamed *Jubilee Bridge*. The destination would usually be *Sandy Gap*, where you could buy jugs of hot water to brew tea. The beach would be crowded as many families went there for the day.

As if things weren't hard enough during this period, tragedy was to strike the family. It was one day in June 1936 that Edwin had gone to Sowerby Wood on his bike, as was his usual wont. He was quite deaf in his right ear, due to being exposed to heavy bombardment during the Great War. On this particular day he had left his bike near to the railway crossing at Sandscale and commenced picking flowers in the hedge near to the railway line that curved around as it came to the crossing. He never returned home from his flower-picking on that fateful summer's night.

From the local police, who returned Edwin's bicycle, the family learnt that he had been struck by the south-bound service, around 10.12pm, on its way to *Barrow Central* as it came around the curve at Sandscale. The police never divulged the fact that Edwin's body had been literally cut in half by the wheels of the locomotive [2]. Furthermore, it was not until the engine arrived into Oldham station later that day, when pieces of flesh were seen on the front of the engine, that the engine

Pte Edwin Stockton, age 18, of the King's Own Royal Lancaster Regiment in 1914.

driver became aware of what had happened. It was not unusual for Edwin to go off alone to pick wild flowers. What was unusual, on this occasion, was the hour. He was killed at roughly 10.15pm, a time when the light would have been fading. Sydney, his eldest son, always maintained that his father had called into the *Ormsgill Hotel* for a drink. This was never validated. Moreover, had alcohol been a factor, then surely this would have emerged at the inquest, where a verdict of accidental death was recorded. Following the inquest and right up to the present day, a 10-mph speed restriction has existed on the south-bound curve at Sandscale. The devastation imposed on the Stockton family by the sudden loss of its bread-winner was immeasurable. Drastic action had to be implemented as Edwin's four children were still at school, so they were split up and 'farmed out' to the wider family. [The widow's pension at the time did not stretch to feeding and clothing four healthy children]. It was agreed that Sydney, the eldest and being 13, would stay in Fell Street with the Johns family, while Joan went to live with Uncle Barney in Sycamore Grove, Jack went to Agnes in Manchester Street and Frank went to the Park family of Pennington, near Ulverston. One of Lizzie's sisters, Ada, had married Frank Park⁵. Help with the Stockton children was not forthcoming from the East Mount side of the family however. The Marshes, obviously, preferring their *days of wine and roses* to those of runny noses! Lizzie was left to deal with her grief.

Life goes on as they say and then two years later Lizzie began to find companionship with neighbour, Jimmy Jones, who lived around the corner in Cavendish Street. The relationship developed and they married.

Jones was a steady, dependable, sort of guy and he had worked as doorman at the Roxy on Cavendish Street and then later at the Coliseum. In fact he managed to get Jack Stockton his first job, upon leaving school, as a reel-winder in the projection room at the Coliseum. Unfortunately, it wouldn't be long before tragedy was to strike once more.

---

⁵ Frank Park ran a haulage business. It was based at Pennington near Ulverston

Marsh's Luxury Radio Coaches in Cavendish Street about to embark on an excursion for local residents. They were parked outside of what, in 2018, is the Cavendish Dental Practice and the Barrow Labour Club. Lizzie Stockton can be seen against the side of the coach, immediately below the third window from the rear. 1936. *Stockton family photo.*

Lizzie died in childbirth at the age of 37. This was in 1939. Following her death, Jones stayed on at 35 Fell Street but the child, who they named Keith, was fostered by his sister who later moved to Warrington, taking Keith with her. As for Lizzie's other children, Sydney went into Vickers as an apprentice shipwright; Joan secured a job as a waitress in the Ritz art deco café before going into Barrow Steelworks. Following his stint in the Coliseum, Jack went into farm service. It is not clear what became of Frank – the youngest sibling. However, soon after, with the outbreak of the Second World War he was evacuated to somewhere around the *Tebay* area, where he stayed for some time.

Sources & Notes to Chapter Two
1 Register of Electors for 1930 and 1931
2 North-Western Daily Mail, 30th June, 1936.
3 Personal communications with Jack and Alan Stockton.
4 The world, in the 1930s, still 'clanged & chuffed', the digital age being well into the future.

Tea Party, Sandy Gap: Children from Fell Street and Cavendish Street. Left to right: Irene Tatham; Syd Stockton; unknown; Bob Waters (standing); Frank Stockton (front); Muriel Tatham; Bill Coward (Manchester Street); Norman Tatham; Joan Stockton; the boy Waters; unknown; Bill Waters and Jack Stockton. 1936. *Stockton family photo.*

Paddling in the sea at Sandy Gap are three ladies from Fell Street;
left to right are Mrs Waters; Mrs Tatham and Mary Elizabeth Stockton. 1936. *Stockton family photo.*

Chapter Three

The 1940s and 50s

My paternal grandparents, John (Jack) Henderson and Hannah Elizabeth Thompson, [both from Maryport, Cumberland], had three known addresses in Barrow. From 1921 their first home in the town was at 12 Arthur Street, followed by a house in Hall Street and then from 1925 at 3 Howe Street, Hindpool which, for several years, was shared with a widow, one Elizabeth Fletcher about whom nothing more is known. This property was rented from local shopkeeper Mr G. Humphries and was next door but one to his shop, which stood at the corner of Bath Street and Howe Street. During the 1940s, as well as selling general provisions, it also traded in animal foodstuffs, as many in those war years kept pigs and poultry on local allotments *(hence Piggy Lane)*. On the opposite corner was *Pearson's* fruit and vegetable shop which later became *Rita's* - but more about this lady later.

Patterson's shop at the corner of Bath Street and Howe Street. It had previously been a branch of Lewis's, originally Messers Humphries. To the left and on the corner of Exmouth Street is Gregory's Off License.

Courtesy of Ron Knight 1973.

My dad, Stanley, was born in Howe Street in October 1925 and he was named after the then Prime Minister, Stanley Baldwin.

Bath Street is the main stem of the area known as Upper Hindpool. During the period under review it was a bustling shopping thoroughfare which ran northward from its junction with Abbey Road and on up to Walney Road. Most of the commerce was conducted on the section between Abbey Road and Blake Street and almost any commodity that local folk needed could be sourced along here. *Alice Leach once told me that in the early years of the town, for a short time, it was a forerunner of Dalton Road i.e. the main shopping thoroughfare.* Ramsden Hall, the Victorian edifice which gave rise to the street's name, still stands at its Abbey Road junction. Originally built as a *plunge* and gifted to the town by the first Mayor, Sir James Ramsden in 1872, it has subsequently been an annexe of Barrow College and is currently a branch of the Citizens Advice Bureau[1].

Number 1 Bath Street was the home of the Brady family. It was also, for many years, the registered office of their business – *Brady's Transport and Warehousing Ltd.* Bob Brady Jnr. was a school colleague and is still a friend. Directly opposite, on a piece of waste land owned by Brady, a guy in a wheelchair would sit watching the world go by and he would greet everyone who passed. His name was George (Furness?) and I assumed him to be a *Great War* veteran. In fact George would be the first thing anyone

saw when turning from Abbey Road into Bath Street, he was, in effect, the street's *Gatekeeper*. On the corner of Bath and Dundonald Streets was a small fruit and vegetable shop *(previously a fish and chip shop)*. This was also owned by Brady and run by Bob's mum Audrey. Further along Bath Street and on a corner with Nelson Street stood the *Furness Hotel*. This large imposing building at 13, was originally owned by brewer, James Thompson & Co.** During the early 1950s it was dad's local, where he played in the darts team. The top man during the 1950s was a Lenny Gidney. On the opposite corner, at 15, stood the pawn shop, complete with brass balls. Throughout the 1950s I thought the proprietor was one of my uncles. Every Monday dad's suit would go in, then on Fridays mum would say, "Here is five bob, go to Uncle Tommy's and redeem your father's suit". To the best of my knowledge my father never knew that the suit he wore at weekends had been in hock all week!

During conversations with steelwork's electrician, Ray Millard, while researching a steelwork's book project, he told me that, when he was at school, just prior to the war, there were several gangs at Hindpool. The toughest, he said, was the Howe Street gang, which comprised the Bromleys; Hendersons; Lavenders and Warriners. He also told me that Howe Street hosted the area's main V.E. Day party in May 1945[3]. Ray had been brought-up in Monk Street where his parents had a small shop called Beatty's. His dad, Sam, was the local barber.

During the Blitz of 1941, the odd-numbered side of Howe Street, from 11 to 55, which included Tommy Dodd's beer shop (off-licence) on the corner of Keye's Street, were flattened – along with parts of Blake and Exmouth Streets. As a temporary measure[1], prefabricated bungalows were erected to ease the housing shortage.

Sometime during the Second World War, all the family, which, as well as Jack and Hannah, included their children John; Dorothy; Stan; William

** James Thompson & Co., a brewer but with no brewery in Barrow.

(Bill) and Elizabeth (Betty), pooled their resources and leased a parcel of land situated at the top of Dane Avenue on the corner with Dalton Lane. [The area nowadays is occupied by the west car park of Furness General Hospital].

On their smallholding, as well as poultry, they ran about 80 pigs (Wessex Saddlebacks). These lovely animals were predominantly a blue-black colour with white front legs and the eponymous white *saddle*. They also had a *Clydesdale* mare called *Blossom* (Dad preferred this breed to *Shires*, having worked with both when he was the horseman at Home Farm, on Walney Island). There was also a *piebald* pony called *Dinah*. Later, in 1949, they bought a 7-cwt van - which I think was a dark blue Ford Thames - much to the relief of Dinah! During the days of the smallholding Hannah collected waste food such as potato peelings and stale bread from neighbours in the streets around Bath Street. Because of this activity she had gained the rather unfeminine tag of *Pig Woman*. Waste food, known as pig swill, was boiled-up daily in a large steam vessel on the Holding. When cooked it was mixed with pig-meal into what was called *crowdie*[††], then fed to the pigs and poultry.

Approximately half an acre of the holding was put to growing vegetables. This ensured that during the lean war years, when rationing was in place, the family had plenty to eat - with any surplus going to the swine. Sometime during 1947, when my parents, Stan and Joan (Stockton), were *courting* – a term used at the time for "being in a relationship" - my mother had gone to the smallholding to do some weeding of the vegetable patch. This was on a Sunday afternoon, a time when families were out walking. My mother, on this particular occasion, remembers wearing a very colourful headscarf. A family, walking along Dane Avenue, stopped to watch the work in progress. "Look", said a little girl to her mother and pointing at my mum, "Gypsies!" Mother, being both surprised and amused, retold the story on numerous occasions.

†† Crowdie; an old Cumberland word.

Joan Stockton lived at 13 Sycamore Grove, Barrow with her family, the Bowmans, and had worked at Barrow Steelworks throughout most of the war years. Sometime in 1947 dad had started back in the hoop department at the steelworks after several years of farm work. They met each other at a dance at the Holker Old Boys club on Bath Street then wed in March the following year, moving into an upstairs flat at No 2 Napier Street. [The flat was above the shop at 18 Bath Street. In 2018 this shop is the Barrow Take Away, once owned by local shopkeeper Florrie Wookey]. They shared the flat with a cousin, Dolly Bowman and her husband Jack (Jed) Bartlett. Then in March 1949 I came along and although the war had been over for four years, food rationing was still in place. Meat and some luxury goods, e.g. chocolate were still in short supply.

Our block on Bath Street, during the 1950s, comprised six retail outlets between Napier and Vernon Streets. There was Wookey's vacant unit (18) under our flat; Foley's cobblers; *Dorothy's* confectioners; *Delamere's* grocers; *Bullock's* sweet shop then *Wookey's* greengrocers. Opposite us on Bath Street was a post office run by Mr & Mrs Gass. Diagonally opposite the post office was Parker's butchers shop. From our front window, the one that overlooked Bath Street, it was possible to see right along Rodney Street and St Mary's church. The nuns were always in evidence along there. Two of the earliest sounds I can remember are the church's two bell chime, also the slamming shut of the pillar box after it had been emptied by the postie.

My baptism took place at St James's church on 15th May, 1949 by the Reverend J. Morton. During the jollifications at the celebratory tea, held afterwards at nanna's house, a fight broke out between my two godfathers, Billy Lavender and Ronny Warriner. Apparently, they had been to the Wheatsheaf prior to the christening and a disagreement had turned into a scuffle. Upon sobering-up later in the day, they made their peace with each other.

The smallholding was broken up sometime after grandad's death in 1951. John and Dorothy, then engaged to be married, needed their shares to enable them to set up their own homes. John, with his wife Doris, bought 49 Monk Street, Hindpool while Dorothy (Dot) stayed at home because, for some obscure reason, her new husband, Eric Rushton, left her literally days after the wedding to go to, it is believed, Canada. Dorothy never recovered and lived like an old maid until, sadly, she died at Roose Hospital in her mid-fifties from muscular dystrophy.

Grandad Jack was 57 when he passed over in 1951. Shortly after, in the September, my sister, Joan Elisabeth, was born. Jack had struggled for years with bronchitis and asthma. He had also been gassed during the First World War, which compounded his chest problem. I would have only been 18 months old when my grandfather died and yet I can always conjure up one memory of him, with his short white hair, in a chair, smoking his pipe. I was so taken with this pipe that, for a bit of peace, he gave me one to keep. I am told that I seldom had it out of my mouth.

When my sister, Joan, was born it was found that she had the same condition that had afflicted our mother – Hip Dysplasia. This is where the socket of the hip bone is not deep enough to fully accommodate the ball at the end of the thigh-bone (femur) which causes it to become dislocated. As a result of this, Joan was sent to an orthopaedic hospital at Windermere for treatment and ongoing management of her condition. The hospital had been called the *Ethel Hedley Hospital for Crippled Children* and situated close to the lake shore, at Calgarth Park. It had originally been a hospital for First World War soldiers.

Visiting posed a problem for my parents as the hospital was off the beaten track with regards to public transport. Shopkeeper, Sammy Bone, whose premises were on the corner of Duke Street and Blake Street and opposite the Queen's Hotel, came to the rescue. Mr Bone had a 1937 Austin

Seven car which he very kindly loaned my parents. I can recall our first visit and being in the vehicle when we were driving along the A592 by the side of Lake Windermere. It was mid-winter on a very foggy evening. The fact that the car had only one headlight working did nothing to help the situation! Then, upon arriving at the hospital, I was not allowed onto the ward to see my sister. The hospital's visiting policy precluded children! So I waited in the reception area in the company of a nurse. Joan spent a total of 18-months at Ethel Hedley, most of the time in traction which, thankfully, corrected her condition. (See Appendix 1: childhood health).

Early in 1952 Uncle Bill was conscripted into the Army for his National Service, where he saw action in Malaya.

Uncle John, dad's elder brother, told me about the time the family bought Blossom at *Appleby Horse Fair* – which was, and still is, a popular event for bucolics and gypsies. John and Bill had gone to Barrow Railway Station to coincide with dad getting back with the horse. According to John, dad went into the horsebox to get Blossom – who was determined not to move – so dad was on the verge of losing his temper when into the box walked uncle Bill with halter in hand, speaking softly to the horse, (Bill always had a way with livestock, probably from his days in farm service at Biggar Village, Walney during the war). With a minimum of fuss, Bill deftly slipped the halter over Blossom's head and led her off the train like they were old friends! The mare was used on the smallholding for ploughing and general arable duties. After the holding was sold she was bought by the Simpson family who had Ormsgill Farm at that time - known to Hindpool children as *Dingle Farm.*

The pony, Dinah, until the van appeared, was used for pulling the two-wheel cart they had. Eggs would be delivered to the egg packing station at 32 Hindpool Road returning *via* the corn mill, loaded with pig meal or crushed oats. It is not known what became of Dinah after the holding was sold.

Sometime in 1952 we left Napier Street and moved into 38 Hood Street. This was a depressing house (possibly because it had lain empty for a while before we moved in). It had no hot water, no power points, no bathroom and only an outside toilet. The street itself was fine, there were some respectable families in Hood Street and I made some good friends. Our next-door neighbours, at 40, was the Keighan family, comprising Willis and Alice with children Brian; Ted; Joan; Ann; Linda; Doreen and Pauline. All in a 2-bedroom terrace! Next to them at 42 were the Stirzakers, widower Alf, his son Ken and also living with them was Bill Pearson, who was a steelworker and also Alf's brother-in-law. Bill was a kind man and was affectionately called *Uncle Willy* by most of the children in the street. The Logan family lived at 44 (Jim Logan was the supervisor at Marshes during the 1960s).

Moving to Hood Street brought us closer to the iron and steel works and from this time onwards I became influenced by its powerful presence. Also at this time I was unaware that my family connection with the place went back to 1876. [For several years I thought the Steelwork's office block – with the Union flag flying - was Hindpool's town hall]. In Hood Street and even while at school on Blake Street, we were living in the shadows of its tall chimneys, rumblings, screaming furnaces and general daily commotion. There was a kind of omnipresent throb and hum. Thirty or so years later, when the works disappeared, it was as though Hindpool had lost its soul.

At the bottom of Hood Street and across Howard Street was Bell's waste paper/coal yard. The Bell family were originally from the Isle of Man.(see appendices) Next to this was Marsh's Aerated Water Factory.

Walter Marsh was born in Derby. His father, William, is listed as being a *pot presser* in the 1871 Census. In 1890 Walter came to Barrow looking for work, which he found at the shipyard, and for a while he worked there as a riveter. In 1891 he is listed as living at 168 Dalton Road, Barrow, with his wife where they rented rooms above a shop. In 1901 they were living at 40 School Street and were letting most of the rooms. One of their lodgers (1901 Census), was an assistant accountant with Vickers Sons and Maxims called Edwin Henry Dance. Mr Dance came from Blackfriars, Central London. The first soft drinks were made in the cellar of this house in School Street (the address was listed as Aerated Water Manufactury). It is generally held by the Stockton family that Edwin Dance had helped Walter establish his business. It is also believed that Dance was instrumental in obtaining the 'secret recipe' for Marsh's Sarsaparilla (the labels on the early bottles displayed the full name. The description 'Sass' did not appear until sometime later). The recipe most likely emanated from the apothecary on Blackfriars Road, London and probably involved a degree of quackery i.e. claims of medicinal value. While living on School Street, Walter and his wife, Margaret, had their first child, Leonard. They also took in a young girl as a domestic. The girl, Mary Bowers, eventually became their adopted daughter.

By 1911 the Marshes were sufficiently buoyant to be able to purchase a large property at 22 Park Drive, Barrow. This house is directly opposite the junction with West Avenue. The location would have been convenient for meeting travelling sales representatives and other business contacts. Edwin Dance also moved into this new house.

During 1921 Walter branched into the motor coach business. The Marshes probably bought their vehicles over a period of time – initially ex-WW1 personnel carriers purchased at a bargain price and then modified and repainted. They garaged some coaches to the rear of 85 Dalton Road and in Fisher's Yard, adjacent to the Kings Arms. Leonard Marsh managed the soft drinks side of the business while younger son, Walter Jnr., looked after the transport and property concern.

The derelict Aerated Water Factory on Duke Street, Barrow.

My recollection of Marshes during the fifties and sixties is one of a thriving business, more so during the summer months when they took on casual labour (usually the boys of Lyon and Hood Streets). They had two delivery trucks, painted black and white in a zebra-style. The factory doors were also in this style. The loaded vehicles would leave the premises *via* the Duke Street exit then return loaded with empties to the Howard Street elevation. Because Howard Street was too narrow for the lorries to make a 90° turn into the factory, they would drive along Lyon Street, which aligned the appropriate access door. The Marsh's logo on the lorry doors was very similar to the *Billy Boy* logo of Lakeland Laundries!

The product range, as I recall, was: around eight flavours of pop, the most popular being Sass, Orange and Lemonade; a robust ginger beer, which came in a squat stone bottle. Several cordials and Soda Syphons for the licenced trade. They also made a malt vinegar (non-brewed condiment).

Name and Surname	Relationship to Head of Family	Age Males	Age Females	Particulars as to Marriage					Profession or Occupation			Birthplace	Nationality	Infirmity
Walter Marsh	Head	41		Married	21	5	2	3	Mineral Water Mfr Dir		own account	Derby 21	English	
Margaret Marsh	Wife		40	Married	21	5	2	3	House Wife		at Home	Manchester 59	English	
Walter Marsh	Son	19		Single					Apprentice Fitter & Turner	689	Employed Worker	Barrow in F.	English	
Leonard Marsh	Son	13		Single					at School 390			Barrow in F.	English	
Mary Bowers	adopted Daughter		16	Single					Help at Home		at Home	Barrow in F.	English	

1911 Census. Cumbria Archives and Local Study Centre (Barrow).

During the 1950s Hannah was adjusting to widowhood. She involved herself with the Salvation Army (the Sally) attending the Home League every Monday and then she became a kind of unofficial recruitment officer for the S.A. Sunday school. I have vivid memories of attending with my sisters Joan and Marjorie and although pressed into going, I have to say that the Sunday school trips and Christmas parties were always very enjoyable events. I can remember singing – "*Sunshine Corner always jolly fine, it's for children under ninety nine, all are welcome come-and-you-will-see, Barrow Sunshine Corner is the place for me.*" Families I remember from Sunday school are: Briars; McGill and McKechnie.

We attended the SA Sunday school right throughout the 1950s - along with other local children – conscripts of my grandmother!

In 1953 dad left the hoop works and went to work for William McLung who was a haulage contractor of North Scale, Walney Island. McLung had a licence to sell sand and gravel which was excavated from the gravel pits of North Walney. These were situated on the western edge of the aerodrome. Access was actually from the aerodrome itself. McLung at the time had two 7-ton diesel tipper lorries. One was a Bedford, the other a Commer. I remember accompanying dad many times when he delivered loads of gravel to Millom ironworks along the A595 which, in those days, for a lorry, was only just passable. We always seemed to use the Commer with a guy called Joe Steel driving the Bedford. We did that run so many times that I am sure the wagon could have found its own way to Millom.

Around this time Jack Stockton came to live with us. Jack, a bachelor, was one of mam's younger brothers. He had previously been living with a work colleague called Eddie Mansell on the Newbarns estate. For a while Jack and I bunked together, in the front bedroom, until mam could afford a single bed for him. In joining the family, Uncle Jack also joined the crew of dad's fishing boat which was a 28-foot converted ship's lifeboat, BW 49, moored on the Ferry Beach and more about this later.

In 1954, the year my sister Marjorie was born, I started school at St. James' Infants (later renamed Brisbane Park Infants School). I recall my first day and seeing a lot of the children crying at being parted from their mums. I was actually alright with it and remember sitting next to one of my friends, Philip Dubka. The Head Mistress was Miss Snowdon, our form teacher was a Miss Cameron who, after becoming Mrs Taylor, also taught us up at big school (the Jimmy's). In subsequent years we were taught by Miss Nevinson and Miss Knight. Both these ladies, who were in their mature years, and probably single, were what I would class as career teachers, totally committed to their calling. They had actually taught my father when he was there. A feature of the school building that is foremost in my memory is the parquet floor, especially in the hall. It was a dazzling geometric design of diagonal oak slats. (I recall that we spent a lot of time sat on this floor). Two other memories from my days at infant school are having the lovely children's book *The Wind in the Willows* by Kenneth Grahame, read to us by Miss Cameron. This story captured my imagination so much that I have read the book twice in subsequent years and, although written in 1908, it remains one of the most enduring of children's stories. The other is being taken in a group onto Blake Street by a visiting policeman called Sergeant Shepherd, and taught our kerb drill.

Teacher's assistant was a very sweet lady we knew as Miss Richards. School nurse, who regularly dosed us with cod liver oil, was Sister McFarlane.

The mid-fifties were a lean time for our family. Dad had gone back into the steelworks as a crane driver, just as the works went onto a 3-day week. During this period I recall that a lot of my clothes came from jumble sales, as did Christmas presents. I always wanted an electric train set but had to be content with a second hand clockwork version‡‡. My school friends seemed to have the electric models, *Triang* and *Hornby-Dublo* being the most popular makes. One school friend in particular was Rodger Ker. Rodger had actually invited me to come to his home, which was 12 Osborne Street, to play with his toys. The front room at his house [called the parlour in these times], had an electric train set permanently set out. His dad, a joiner at the shipyard, had built the wooden trestles upon which the model stood. Additionally, Rodger had an impressive collection of *Dinky* toys and *Meccano* as well as the current range of board games such

‡‡ Whenever I asked for something financially 'out of reach' my request would be countered with "Good God Stanley, you will have us in the workhouse!

as *Waddington's Monopoly* and *Scoop*. I suppose being an only child, his parents could afford to provide so many nice things for him! I spent some very enjoyable times at their home in Osborne Street, quite often having tea there. Rodger's mam, a homely Scottish lady called Annie, was the 'British Standard' mum and housewife of the fifties – always at home and always baking. [It was 40 years later that I discovered the Ker's house was the birth-place of my grandfather, Edwin Stockton].

I recall being taken to Craven Park during the mid-fifties. This would be on Saturday afternoons. Dad always liked to watch the game from the covered terraces at the Clive Street end of the Park. Sometimes there would be so many spectators that he would have to put me onto his shoulders so that I could see the game. I felt sure the attraction was Willie Horne - has there ever been a better stand-off in League or Union?

Both of my parents were serious smokers, dad smoked a pipe and also took snuff at work, at home he smoked cigarettes with mam – who was a twenty per day user (Capstan, sometimes Capstan Full Strength, which I would get for her from Ted Davies' shop). Looking back they always seemed to have money for their addiction, while my sisters and I lived off fried bread and sometimes sugar sandwiches. [The Keighan girls, next door, always seemed to prefer brown sauce on their piece]. Ted Davies had the shop at 23 Bath Street. Ted's, as we called it, had previously been run by the Starrets, it sold mainly sweets and tobacco. Ted was a quiet, unassuming, mustachioed little chap. His wife, Mary, originated from Oldham and she retained a pronounced Lancashire accent. They were a very private couple who kept to themselves. I remember they had a Ford Prefect car, this model had only three forward gears and a single windscreen wiper that was air-driven. The vehicle only came out of its garage once per week – on Sunday evenings – when the shop was closed. [Many years later I was to discover that Ted Davies, this quiet little shopkeeper from my childhood, had been an accomplished RAF fighter-pilot during the war!].

Despite the hardship and privations[§§] of the 1950s we somehow managed to get a television set. This coincided with the launch of *Granada* Television in 1956. I believe we were one of the first in Hood Street to have one and because our house had no electric sockets, the set had to be powered from a double adaptor, plugged into the light socket with the flex taped across the ceiling and down the wall. Every afternoon, around tea-time, school friends would knock asking if they could come in to watch *Children's Hour.*

Through the 'new' medium of television I was introduced to the Golden Age of Hollywood. The routine became, when dad was on afternoon shift, that Aunty Dolly (dad's sister) would come down to our house where we would watch the weekly film - usually through a haze of cigarette smoke. Films of the 1930s, such as *The 39 Steps* with Robert Donat; *Mutiny on the Bounty* starring Charles Laughton also *The Hunchback of Notre Dame* were having their first airing on British television. And then later, Humphrey Bogart vehicles, including the 1940s film noir genre. Our evenings would conclude with yours truly being sent out for fish suppers. During the period under review there were four options viz – Whittaker's on the corner of Keyes Street and Howe Street, Schofield's were at the top of Parry Street. Whitall's and May's were in Lower Hindpool. Whitall's on Calcutta Street with May's at 2 McClintock Street. We tended not to use May's because of the rumours. Mr May would spend an inordinate amount of time in the back of his shop, leaving customers waiting. Allegedly shoving his haemorrhoids back. The saying was – "Always go to May's because you get piles of chips!" My destination was invariably Whitall's - because the offering there was toothsome. The woman here was a stout lady called Bessie, as well as serving she also had to fry and keep the coal-fired range going. This shop, on Calcutta Street, had previously been a pay-office of the Barrow Haematite Steel Company and was where men, who were on short-term contracts, collected their wages.

§§ Around this time we would have people calling for money every week eg the rent man, coal man and insurance man. There would be some weeks when finances wouldn't stretch to paying them all. My parents system was to put all creditors' names in a hat. If we owed, say, six people but could only afford to pay four of them then the first four names out of the hat would be paid. If the unfortunate two became shirty, Pop politely told them if they upset him their names wouldn't even go into the hat!

My recall of the Scotch Buildings is scant given I was only seven years old when demolition work started in May 1956. They had been built by the Steel Company but in 1932 sold off to a housing association. I can remember wandering through once they had been vacated by residents and so I saw for myself the standard of accommodation they provided. I have many friends who were brought up in the Buildings and all report happy memories. Mainly from the good neighbour and community spirit aspect. Ken Royall moved into 304f, a top-floor flat on Duke Street, in 1948. He said the drawback with being on the upper level was when you needed to draw water when someone below had the same idea. Your tap would just gurgle. The system used by top-floor tenants was to keep a large spoon near the sink, this would then be used to 'rap on your tap', signifying to those below your need for water.

Work colleague Tommy Livesey's only recall, as a child, is of being in bed and hearing the mouse traps going off, also the clatter of men's clogs on the slate pavements outside as they made their way to the steelworks for 6am.

The proprietor of Rita's shop [36 Bath Street], was Margarita Rosewarne, who was married to Raymond, a television repair man with *Rediffusion*. Rita was cast in the same mould as Uncle Willy and, like him, had no children of her own. One of the treats that we enjoyed with her was being taken to the cinema on Saturday afternoons. I recall being taken, along with David and Keith Reynolds; Philip Dubka and Chrissy Green to Barrow's Odeon to see - *Cockleshell Heroes; Forbidden Planet* and two Fess Parker *Davy Crockett* films. Fess Parker became a childhood hero and *via* the *Davy Crockett* franchise his films spawned a thriving spin-off industry as the shops became stocked with *Davy Crockett* themed items. Mother made me a realistic *Davy Crockett* hat from an old fox-fur which she had managed to get from one of her jumble sales.

During the late 1950s, Hannah secured a position at *Middleton Tower* holiday camp (later to become part of the Fred Pontin Empire) which was south of Heysham and near to Morecambe where she worked as a domestic. She would be 65 years old at the time. Middleton Tower was a very popular holiday destination in those days – as was Morecambe itself and I have many fond memories of times spent at both places. I remember asking dad if we could maybe visit Blackpool for a change sometime. His reply was in the negative, saying that we weren't missing anything. Many years later I determined that, of the two resorts, Morecambe was preferable, being more friendly (there always seemed to be intoxicated and unsavoury characters about in Blackpool and anyway, it didn't have the lovely view across the water that Morecambe had).

From the age of eight I started going to the *Ritz* cinema on Saturday mornings. Usually, there would be a group of us – the Reynolds brothers, Chrissy Green, and Joan Shepherd - who lived on Nelson Street. The Ritz, during the 50s, had become the ABC. We attended the ABC Minor's club and it was fantastic! Two of the cinema staff that I recall are, the assistant manager, a Greek guy, called Mr Fotis. The bouncer – if that's the proper term – was Jim Ainsbury known widely as Jimmy Niff-Naff. This was because of a speech impediment he had but it didn't detract from his engaging personality. I have some happy memories of being an ABC minor and at 6d admission, it was excellent value!

The year 1956 also saw an upturn in the family finances. What happened was, while being on short time working up at the steelworks, dad secured a part-time job for himself. This was with John (Joe) Binnell who was a local contractor and scrap metal dealer situated on Barrow Island. Binnell had taken on more than he could handle – at the time he was demolishing the Hindpool Scotch Buildings – which took the focus away from his Marine Store, located on North Road, directly opposite the entrance to the Graving Dock, which nowadays is the *Dock Museum*. Dad was placed in charge of this part of the business. Binnell had two 5-ton petrol tipper lorries. One a Bedford, the other a Dodge. These wagons were not kept in good repair (unlike those of William McLung). I recall that neither would start without being towed and they would also frequently overheat. One memorable outing was where we were taking a load of scrap cast iron to the ironworks at Backbarrow in the Bedford. This was during the period when Barrow Council were replacing the old gas street lighting with electric. Binnell had bought all the cast iron lamp posts. On this particular day we had loaded-up at the Corporation Yard, which was accessed off

Marsh Street, and with extra cans of water to top-up the radiator, headed out of town. The layout at Backbarrow was such that the ironworks were on a much lower level than the A590 and was accessed by a cinder track down a steep gradient. And as there was insufficient room local to the blast furnace bunker to turn around, you had to reverse down the gradient. Dad insisted that I alight while he made the manoeuvre. Seconds later I heard a shout as father leapt from the cab leaving the truck to career down the slope and crash into the bunker, where it immediately discharged its cargo. The truck's brakes had failed!

As well as the ironworks, Backbarrow was famous for its Blue Mills (Dolly Blue); this was a pigment used in laundering. The factory, which was owned by Reckitt and Coleman, had originally been an 18th century cotton mill. Dolly Blue was widely distributed. Jack Stockton worked for Athersmith Bros haulage contractors during the '50s, he recalls transporting regular loads of China Clay (a constituent of Dolly Blue) to Backbarrow from the Firm's sister depot in Hull.

Things improved again when, in 1958, dad moved onto the experimental continuous casting plant at the steelworks, which meant a substantial increase in pay. Because of this he was able to get himself a little Ford 8 van, which he bought from *Stollers Furniture Store*. Stoller traded from a shop on Dalton Road in those days. We could now enjoy trips along the coast road (A5087), where we would walk out on the beach and, occasionally, harvest cockles.

Once a week we would have faggots for tea from Jeavon's pork shop[¶¶] on Anson Street *(Jeavon's shop was directly opposite Richardson's bakery [116], which, incidentally, had been the birthplace of Sir Leonard Redshaw's mother – Ada)*. Faggots, also known as savoury ducks, are best described as giant meatballs and at the time they cost fourpence each. Mother would place these in an oven-proof dish with water then bake them for around 40-minutes. The result was the most toothsome, culinary delight that

¶¶ Smells from the 1950s, no longer with us and recalled by the author, include – the aroma emitted from the pork shop as the daily fare was being processed; fish and chips being fried with dripping; fresh bread being made in the local bakeries and also the smell of damp news-print in an outside lavatory.

hungry young mouths could experience, and the gravy was to die for! I would later discover that my favourite tea was an amalgam of minced pork, liver, onion, herbs and spices wrapped in a caul [lamb's afterbirth].

Whilst the faggots were a good buy, other of Jeavon's products were not! The pork sausages were something my mother avoided. Sausage in those days were traditionally made with ground meat mixed with a proportion of rusk (biscuit meal). It was said the Jeavon's sausages comprised more rusk than meat! So much so that Father McKenna of St Mary's Church turned a blind eye when members of his flock ate Jeavon's sausage on Fridays!

By 1959 I was coming to the end of my time at junior school, which was St James C of E Junior School on Blake Street. The Jimmy's was a good school - education-wise - but a very strict one. Moreover, we were also taught national values and elements of good citizenship. I always termed it quasi-military as we always seemed to have to march everywhere and would be drilled on the playground, in response to a whistle. School life was governed by a rigidly enforced set of rules, and the ringing of a hand-held bell. The Queen's English was sacrosanct and we were discouraged from using words in their abbreviated form. On one occasion I was chastised for casually using the word pub! Another rule was that we weren't to use American English. The diktat being– "do not confound the language of the Nation with words of –osity and – ation", e.g. medicine and not medication.

The highlight of the academic year was the Bowker Essay. This was a literary competition, conceived in memory of Robert Bowker, the school's first Head Teacher and entered into by every pupil with the winner having his/her name appended to a scroll which was displayed on the wall of the school hall under Mr Bowker's portrait. Two winners that I remember are: John Saddler (Cook Street) and Janice Dubka (Anson Street).

The Head Teacher, Pop Denmead (successor to Mr Anthony), along with his staff, had no sense of humour – certainly not in my view. Between them they "knocked chunks" out of me. Implements of torture were, apart from the official cane, a pair of wooden blackboard compasses; a gym shoe and a bunch of 12-inch wooden rulers banded together. However, for my money, by far the worst experience was meted out by Mr York.

Pop York would pull up the leg of your [short] trousers and literally slap the back of your bare thigh until it was deep red. This would be after dragging you, by the ear, from your desk to the front of the class (teachers knew how to inflict pain without leaving evidence of their assault on your person). I believed that he took pleasure from his actions as the victim would squirm and contort whilst in his clutches. You were left with the feeling that this man truly hated you. Another tartar was Miss Whitham, who would suddenly strike you, without warning, full-force across your face. I recall being on the receiving end during an RI lesson. The Jimmy's was what was termed in those days 'High Church' with Religious Instruction high on the agenda. We were taught the Nicene Creed until we could recite it backwards. We were not told that it had been the brain-child of the, hitherto, pagan Roman Emperor, Constantine the Great.

[Friends who attended St Mary's RC school on Howard Street (the Mary's), reported no easier time, the nuns there, apparently, could also be slap-happy].

There was one teacher who I must praise – Mr Shaw – a lovely man. Pop Shaw had not come from academic origins, he had been what used to be termed a dilutee, coming into the profession just before the war. Mr Shaw was a 'natural' with a big heart. He was soccer mad and an ardent supporter of Barrow AFC. He was also a very keen fell-walker whose enthusiasm fuelled my own interest in the activity. I recall our first outing, which was in 1958, where he took a group of us up Black Combe. Despite being a short man, he could set a very brisk pace.

The vicar, the Reverend C P Stannard[***] was always in attendance at morning assembly with his curate, Mr Lofthouse. (Lofthouse was succeeded by Eric Nottman, later to be vicar of St. John's on Barrow Island). The curates lived in the prefab bungalow at 15 Howe Street. Lofthouse was also not averse to throwing his weight around. On one occasion we had to repeat a liturgical ritual which went, thus: *"Thou shalt love the Lord thy God with all thy heart and with all thy soul and with all thy mind - for the Lord thy God is a jealous God"*. On this particular occasion I foolishly

***

[***] Rev Stannard; left St James in 1964 to become Archdeacon of Carlisle.

substituted jealous with jelly and thus incurred Witham's wrath. It was no use telling dad when I got home because he would have given me a crack as well! It was not until years later would I learn that all this punishment was illegal! The only official corporal punishment allowed in schools was *via* the regulation cane – with the use of same recorded in the punishment book. CP in state schools was finally banned, by a vote of parliament, in 1986.

It was also sometime during 1959 that dad upgraded from the Ford 8 van. He bought a 1947 Morris 10 car from Councillor Eric Grayson who was also his boss at the steelworks at the time. I still recall the registration, JWB 646. It was a nice little car with leopard skin seat covers. How can I still remember the registration? Because I washed and polished it so often, that's how!

Other events of 1959 included being enrolled into Furness Judo Club. (Judo is a Japanese martial art which, 5-years later, would be accepted as an Olympic sport). The Dojo was on the Strand in an old building called the Assembly Rooms and next door to the Harbour public house. Club time for juniors was Thursday nights, 7pm until 9pm, then on Saturdays, 10am to 12 noon. Later in the year dad made his foray into whippet racing. [Another activity involving dogs is Hound Trailing and prior to going with the whippets, Hound Trailing was considered. We attended a Trail at Ulpha in the Duddon Valley and although enjoyable, determined that because hounds needed to be walked up to 5-miles a day, the whippet option was more practical]. He had bought a pedigree dog from a guy called Huitson who lived in McClintock Street, Lower Hindpool. The dog, which we called Jasper, was given the racing name Ploughboy. It ran every Thursday, on the track, at Dungeon Meadow, Roose. A year or so later, we would also attend race meetings at Askam; Dalton; Millom and Whitehaven.

It was also in 1959 that we learnt of the death of Ironworks boss, William Killingbeck. Mr Killingbeck had been in London when he suffered a fatal heart attack. His funeral was an almost State affair, being attended by all the district's industrial leaders, financial institutions and professional people.

The list of mourners in the *Barrow News* read like an entry in *Who's Who* for North Lancashire. One mourner not listed, was Killingbeck's personal secretary, Katherine Dorr. (See Appendices).

My last recall of the fifties is going with my school friends into Barrow Shipyard, in November 1959, to watch the launch of England's largest passenger liner, the TSS Oriana, by the tall and elegant Princess Alexandra. I found the occasion a most breath-taking and spectacular event! The man who has become blasé about seeing dynamic ship launches must be a peculiar and dull fellow, or is not yet born[4]. The poet Longfellow sums it up nicely -

> *And see! She stirs!*
> *She starts, - she moves, - she seems to feel!*
> *The thrill of life along her keel,*
> *And spurning with her foot the ground,*
> *With one exulting joyous bound,*
> *She leaps into the ocean's arms!*

1957 and a group of 10-year old pupils photographed outside of St James' Junior School.

Backr row, left to right are – Barry Woodall; Brian Moore; John Baker; Ray Bromley; Kenny Bray; Colin Burns; Miss Allinson; John Begley; Tommy Clamp; unknown; Jimmy Hollywell. Middle row – unknown; Clive Lowther; Cora Wade; Valerie Dearden; Marilyn Castle; Cath Parker; Shirley Clark; unknown; Malcolm Aird. Front row – Alan Fitzsimmons; Glennis Chelton; Elaine Burgess; Janet Rogers; unknown; Pat Weall; Pauline Round; Jacqueline Huitson; Diane Bowron; Maureen Brown and Arthur 'Baldy' Graham. For some uncool reason most of the boys kept their top shirt button fastened.

Sources & Notes to Chapter Three

1 How Barrow was built: Bryn Trescatheric, 1985.
2 Furness and the Industrial Revolution: D J. Marshall, 1958.
3 Our Barrow (Part 3), Hindpool: Alice Leach, 1980.
4 Paraphrased from Origins, Orient and Oriana; Charles F. Morris, 1980.
5 Personal communications with Bob Brady of Brady's Transport and Warehousing;
Ray Millard, ex-Barrow Steelworks and John Saddler, Cook Street.

An aerial view, from the early '60s, of the developing Hawcoat estate. Dunlop House is in the top r h corner, with Abbey Road cutting across diagonally. Dane Avenue runs from right to left to its junction with Dalton Lane. The location of Henderson's smallholding is bounded by a dark hedge almost centre of image. The fields beyond are now occupied by the Furness General Hospital. *Aerofilms*

Post World War Two; Walney Channel, the Iron and Steelworks and Hindpool stretching into the distance. *Aerofilms, 1947*

The Furness Hotel viewed from the corner of Napier Street. This imposing, well maintained, building in 2018 trades as **Cunninghams**. It remains a popular destination. *S. Henderson, 2018.*

Barrow's rapid growth in the 19th century had not escaped the notice of contemporary journalists, and the
insobriety of its 'immature workers'. There was frequent reference to the 'hard-drinking' local workforce. Such was the concern for Hindpool that a conveyance contained the provision "no public house should be erected in Nelson Street". Some years later the stipulation was waived and – in the perhaps unfair and biting
words of a local solicitor – "the great care for public morality was sold by the Duke of Devonshire and the Furness Railway Company for the sum of £34. 19s, when James Thompson bought it to build a public house.
(The Furness Hotel). Ref.1

Licensees
1920 to 1934: Mr W. Dodd
1935 to 1940: Mr J W Atkinson
1941 to 1949: Mr J J Turner
1950 to 1965: Mr W. Barker

The Pawn Shop at 15 Bath Street (minus brass balls). *S. Henderson 2018.*

Dulce Domum. The upstairs flat at 2 Napier Street at the junction with Bath Street, the shop premises to the left, during the 50s and 60s, was a Heath's off-licence. *S. Henderson 2018.*

St James' County Infants school, (currently Brisbane Park Infants), on Blake Street. *S. Henderson 2018.*

The Salvation Army Citadel (Sunshine Corner) on Collingwood Street. This is the rear of the building, the front entrance being on Abbey Road. It was officially opened on 10th August, 1910. *S. Henderson, 2018.*

The Curate's domicile, 15 Howe Street (mustard front door). *M. Garforth, 1975*

The junction of Exmouth Street and Hartington Street. The 'temporary' prefab bungalows can be seen prior to demolition. *M.Garforth, 1980*

Demolition of Scotch Flats in May, 1956. Binnell's Bedford truck is at the junction of Duke Street and Walney Road. *Courtesy of K.E.Royall.*

Mid 1960s and a group of Hindpool women boarding a coach, in Exmouth Street, for a day excursion. On the bus step is Mrs Doakes. Centre of photo, 7th from right, is Mary Davies (Ted's wife) from Davies' shop at 23 Bath Street. *Courtesy of Darren Gardner.*

Perspective drawing of the Odeon cinema at the junction of Cavendish and Dalkeith street.
One of Barrow's two luxury cinemas. It had originally been the Royalty theatre then later becoming the
Roxy. On the opposite corner is Fallowfield's bakery, later the Tudor Café, *Courtesy of Lynne Corcoran.*

The Dundonald Street elevation of St Mary's R.C. School. The foundation stone was laid in 1871 by Sir James Ramsden, and it officially opened on August 1st 1872. The priest during the mid-sixties was Canon J. McKenna, MBE – he of kindly face. Two friends from my boyhood who attended the school are Brian Shepherd and Michael Salmon. Both aspired to senior positions within VSEL, Barrow. *Courtesy of M. Garforth.*

An early photo of St James C of E Junior School, on Blake Street.
A part of Adelaide Street can be seen in the distance. The school was built on a 3-acre field called Near Greenhill, which was the highest point of the Hindpool lands. It was completed in 1867 and officially opened on January 14th of that year. *Courtesy of Barrow Library.*

A view of the prefabs from Hartington Street with St James' church dominating the scene.
One of the many things missed upon leaving Hindpool to live on Walney Island in 1970, was the church's 8-bell chime.
"We are the best bells in the town". This could be enjoyed every Friday around 7.30pm (Bell-ringing practice).
M. Garforth, 1980.

St James' teachers
Mr York (left);
unidentified youngster
and Mr Shaw.
D. Gardner, 1970s.

Hood Street ladies enjoying the Coronation Day celebrations in 1937.
the photo was taken from the street's junction with Howard Street. *Darren Gardner.*

The Low Road (North Road) which connected Hindpool with Barrow Island.
Courtesy of Cumbria Archives and Local Studies Centre (Barrow)

Chapter Four

The Early Sixties

My earliest recollection of the new decade is of messing about in boats. *Believe me, there is nothing – absolute nothing – half so much worth doing as simply messing about in boats[1].*

As mentioned in the previous chapter, we had a fishing boat on *Ferry Beach[2]*. This had been acquired in 1952 from *Messrs Ward*, ship breakers, who operated at the Barrow side of Devonshire Dock. It was usual in these times for Ward to sell off all the lifeboats from a ship being broken, for the sum of £1 per linear foot. Would-be enthusiasts then set about building up and outfitting their purchase until it became a yacht, cabin cruiser or whatever. Dad, along with his three boating partners – Norman Adams; Major Bromley and Maurice Gifford - were fortunate to obtain a craft that had undergone some preliminary outfitting and, at the time of the purchase, was deployed by Ward as a runabout in Devonshire Dock. The vessel came already engined. It had a four-cylinder *Morris Navigator* marine petrol engine which propelled it along at a good 5-knots, at the time making her the fastest of her class on the Channel. I recall that when we had to change the engine to the more economical two-cylinder *Kelvin*, a bigger propeller was needed. This new item was cast for us in *Grundy's Metal Foundry*. This place was located in what used to be *Hindpool Farm*, on North Road. [It was, perhaps, Hindpool's oldest surviving building]. *I can remember dad taking a bag of pongo to be melted down for the new*

* Pongo: a name given to non-ferrous scrap metal by those in the trade, which included the local rag and bone man.

Grundy's Metal Foundry on North Road, previously Hindpool Farm.
Sometime during 1880 the buildings of Hindpool Farm were taken over by one James Higginson and converted into a brass foundry. Machinery and other tackle being transferred from his original works at Strand, on the dock side and near to the High-Level Bridge. The building on the left was the original farmhouse which was badly damaged during the 1942 blitz, rendering it uninhabitable. The place has been successively - Higginsons; Cookes then Grundy & Stoddarts. Chief brass moulder during the 1950s was Jim Logan of Hood St. When Grundy eventually closed down, Jim secured a position for himself at Caird's Foundry. The LMS horse track is just visible. *Photo 1956 Courtesy J. Melville.*

propeller, which, being unofficial, was done as what was termed a 'foreigner'
in those days.

I spent a lot of my time on Ferry Beach during the early 1960s, usually with Uncle Jack and occasionally Norman Adams, working on the Falcon [BW 49], careening and then painting, as dad's partners seemed to lose interest once the novelty had worn off. They had taken the boat to Fleetwood and Glasson Dock during the 1950s and then realised there was more work than pleasure involved than originally thought.

I have some fond memories of trips in the Falcon, such as trawling in Ulverston Channel, Morecambe Bay, spinning for mackerel in the Irish Sea, about 3 miles off the west coast of Walney and line-fishing (kebbing) on The Flats. This was an area in Morecambe Bay and was located by

An early post card depicting Ferry Beach, the town's (once) main industry is in the background.

steaming, for twenty minutes at about 5-knots, from *Seldom Seen* buoy towards *Blackpool Tower* and then dropping anchor.

The water in this area was crystal clear and on good days you could see the fish (plaice if you were lucky) swimming up from the bottom to take your bait.

There were also family days out on *Piel Island* when my mother and sisters came along. *Piel* was a very popular destination in summer. On one occasion I recall seeing television personality Hughie Green, who, along with his entourage, had sailed across from Peel, Isle of Man and commandeered the bar of *The Ship Inn*.

In 1960 I became a pupil of Holker County Secondary School, which was situated on Holker Street between Milton and Dryden Streets. It had been built in 1875 by local contractor, William Gradwell and opened on January 10th, 1876[3]. Boys and girls attended the school up until 1935 when the local Education Authority decided to move the girls up to Victoria school at Thorncliffe. From then the school was renamed Holker Central Boys Senior School with Mr Kendall Sawrey as Headmaster.

The Head Teacher, in my time there, was George Vaughan, aka the Gaff. [I always thought he resembled veteran actor, Miles Malleson], who had gained the somewhat disrespectful tag of strap-back, apparently because of a corset he was forced to wear to alleviate a chronic back problem. Mr Vaughan always maintained an aloofness which was characterised by a set and serious countenance – body language which told you he was not approachable!

The autumn term that year had started with a change to the school uniform. The original green blazer and grey cap giving way to a black blazer with a new design of badge. The cap was abandoned, although a collar and tie was compulsory and grey flannel trousers were preferred to denim jeans. Unlike the Jimmy's, we could now wear long pants!

I found that only we fags, or freshmen,[9] tended to present in uniform, along with some of the fifth form.

The school day started at 8.50am and prefects were posted at the Milton Street gate to apprehend and log any late arrivals. These officials would also routinely search late-comers for sweets and cigarettes – which they would duly confiscate.

On the first day of term I walked to school with Dave Reynolds, with whom I had come through Infant school and who had been a friend since first moving into Hood Street. Our route to school was, first, onto Anson Street, then turning right into Hartington Street. This wide thoroughfare represented the bourgeois side of Hindpool. With its tree-lined pavements and larger type of terraced house, it is home to the practices of doctors, dentists, veterinarians and others of that ilk. Definitely very 'bay window', it is more an avenue than a street. Our walk to school took us past the *Primitive Methodist chapel* and then the *King's Hall.* This, noble Edwardian, building with its imposing 180-feet long façade facing Hartington Street is of red brick construction trimmed and interspersed with a multiplicity of sandstone mullions and lintels. It was designed, in 1902, by Henry Fowler of Cornwallis Street, Barrow. The main entrance to the building is at the junction of Hartington and Nelson Streets, directly opposite the Alexander Veterinary Centre (originally *Fallowfield's* bakery which had been destroyed in the Blitz, then later rebuilt as a Co-op butchers).

The *Lesser Hall,* immediately next door, was constructed of limestone and had been built years earlier by stone mason, James Garden.

The King's Hall on Hartington Street, Barrow's answer to Carnegie Hall? It once attracted international singers and musicians such as baritone, John Heddle Nash and piano duo - Rawicz and Launder. At the other end of the scale I can recall Wheatsheaf compere, Vic Dempsey, giving a piano recital in the late 1950s. *Frith postcard C. 1910.*

The King's Hall Cupola seen across the roof-tops of Nelson Street during the 1970s. *Courtesy of M.Garforth.*

Construction work started in 1905 and it was opened by the Mayor on 12th September, 1907 with a luncheon for 300-guests held in the *Lesser Hall*. Over the decades the King's Hall has been used as a Methodist Sunday school; a picture house; youth club, venue for military displays; apprentice prize giving events; boxing matches and concerts. It has certainly fulfilled its civic duty to the people of Hindpool. After being the textile factory of *Wood Harris & Co* during '60s and 70s, the premises are currently (in 2019) owned by *Furness Gymnastic Club*, who have undertaken substantial internal repairs.

The auditorium of the King's Hall in 2018, viewed from the gallery. *Photo S. Henderson.*

Continuing on our way, we next turned left, passing Lyon's chemist shop, into Drake Street, where, at *Pickerings* corner shop, for thruppence, we would buy one cigarette and a match - which we would share. This, then, with the odd exception, would be our routine for the next four years.

Our first morning assembly was an eye-opening experience. My first observation was to notice how unlike the Jimmy's it was, where you dare not do more than breath! Such was the control the staff had over you there. Here, there was coughing, mumbling and shuffling of feet - a definite feeling of restlessness.

The school building appeared dated and tired and the hall was only just large enough to accommodate morning assembly, which comprised about 300 pupils. There were outside toilets, situated at the Milton Street end of the school yard, the door to each trap being heavily scarred with years of carved-in graffiti.

Alma Mater; Holker Street School front entrance viewed from Holker Street.
The building on the right was the original gymnasium. *Courtesy of Cumbria Archives and Local Studies Centre (Barrow).*

Once the school body had assembled, Mr Vaughan would appear, attired in his gown (but never his cap). He mounted the stage, which was shared with Assistant Head, Mr Wheeler. Wheeler, who I later found was actually called Albert, was always referred to as Bert during my time at the school. He was a large fellow and in his 60s and he was definitely more of a Bert than an Al. He taught science and music and was also the conductor of the school orchestra and brass band. Also on stage was music teacher, Mr Osborne and a pupil chosen to deliver the day's reading – which was, usually, some bright piece of philosophy for our delectation. This setting could have been straight out of *Tom Brown's School Days.*

Following the Gaff's 'Good morning boys', the band struck up and everyone sang the school paean – 'These things shall be a loftier race[4]'. During which, Dave and I had to stifle our laughter as we took in the grimaces of Mr Osborne, the Gaff's po-face and Bert's habit of playing pocket billiards in full view of the assembled throng. This wasn't a scene from *Tom Brown's School Days*, it was more like the trailer for a 1930s Will Hay comedy!

I have to say that, in all honesty, once I got used to the place and its eccentricities, I did get a good education. Punishment, however, whilst almost as severe as St James', was carried out in a totally different way [apart from what was meted out by George Vaughan]. It was done with a degree of humour – this is not a contradiction. As an example, PE master, Mr Helm would always reserve punishment until the end of his lesson. Before being allowed to get dressed, victims would form a line and bend over, attired only in cotton shorts. Helm would get his size 8 plimsoll and, probably like the rest of us, brain-washed by years of our, rather, pedestrian orchestra and using our backsides as percussion instruments, set about whacking us to the tonic sol-fa. Occasionally, if he believed you deserved more 'medicine,' stopping to include a degree of syncopation (so you might get three whacks instead of one). All this was done much to the amusement of the rest of the class, as they knew the slipper to hurt more when the recipient wore only thin shorts. Another teacher's methods I recall are those of history master Dinkle Downing, who also taught basket weaving. Dinkle would 'cane' you with one of the basket canes – about 5 millimetres diameter. The thing with these was that not only did you feel it across your backside, it would also wrap around you and whack the front of your thigh as well, after which Dinkle insisted that you thanked him.

At the end of assembly we filed out of the hall to a military march played by the band. The form room for class 1A was right next door to the school hall and so we didn't have far to go. About forty of us queued outside of the door until our form teacher, Mr Johnson, arrived. *Nicely*, as he was known, was the double of 1950's actor Richard Wattis. He taught R.I. and English. He lived at 91 Hartington Street with his wife, Hilda, who worked on the cosmetics counter of Lyon's chemist.

Our first task, after the customary introductions, was to make a copy of our timetable. Unlike St James,' we had a different teacher for each subject. Each lesson was about thirty-five minutes duration with a double lesson pro rata. [A breakdown of the school faculty, along with streaming of pupils, can be found in the Appendix].

Another aspect of being at senior school and one I had to get used to, was the ringing of an electric bell every thirty minutes to signify lesson changeover, during which the school corridors became like Euston Station, until everyone became resettled.

Following an induction we headed for our first lesson. This was double maths with Mr Palmen, whose classroom overlooked the rear of the Ritz cinema on Dryden Street. (We had been warned about this guy but were totally unprepared for what happened at this first encounter). Upon being stationed at our desks, Palmen walked slowly to the back of the class, stopping at the desk of Dave Peart. Peart, at six-feet, was easily the tallest in our group, he was a personable lad and neatly turned out in his new uniform. Suddenly, Palmen grabbed the lad's tie, yanking his head down to desk-top level. Then, with shirt buttons pinging, he spun Dave around, grabbing his upper arms then kneeing him in the back. The look of terror on Peart's face said it all – you don't mess with Palmen! During the assault, Palmen never uttered a single word, after which he returned to his desk. I remember taking an instant dislike to this man.

Around 30-years old and standing about five feet five inches tall, Felix Palmen was a stocky guy with a stooped posture, long arms and an expressionless face. He always put me in mind of celebrated actor Sir Donald Wolfit. The ironic thing was, that whilst apparently abhorring bullying, he was the school's number one bully! He was a maths teacher first and foremost, never becoming involved in games, PE, or sports day. Outside of school he was involved with St Matthew's scout troop.

Following his macho display with a 12-year old, Palmen made himself comfortable in his chair, saying, "There's a thick, green book under your desks, turn to page 203 and complete exercise 14". He then sent one of the class out to the school tuck shop, which was on the corner of Milton Street, for a half-pound of Lucky Numbers. Sitting in his chair, apelike, he would then feed his face with sweets until the end of the lesson. [And if he caught you eating sweets during lesson, he would expect you to share with him, you could then continue munching but if you refused to share, he would confiscate what you had]. Palmen never, in my memory, did any 'teaching.' He never engaged us or attempted to draw on our opinion or views. I believe his style responsible for my under-achieving in maths. I was too scared to approach him.

Lessons with *Nicely* were enjoyable experiences. Unlike Palmen, you could sense that this guy had time for you. He would always make the subject of his lectures enjoyable, imbuing what he taught you with instances from his own life experiences. His lessons in Religious Instruction were in total contrast to the indoctrination we received at St James'. Throughout our first term, *Nicely* Johnson set about systematically demolishing our sacred cows!

First year English at Holker was unusual, in that it was a mix of both literature and language. I particularly enjoyed poetry. Again, this was made more interesting by Mr Johnson as he explained what the various poets were trying to say in the context of the language of their period, including the use of metaphor and allegory. He also introduced us to the work of Francis Turner Palgrave[5].

During my first year at senior school my parents took an interest in what I was being taught. I was to discover that they both shared my interest in poetry, mother's favourite being Old Meg[6]: *"Old Meg she was a gypsy, and lived upon the Moors, her bedding was the bright heath turf, her house was out of doors. . . ."*

Dad's was The Vagabond[7]: *"Give to me the life I love, Let the lave go by me, give the jolly heavens above, and the by-way nigh. . . ."*

Vickers work colleague, Gordon Jones, who attended Holker from 1947 to 1952 remembers French lessons: *"PE teacher, in my time, was Mr Turner, a lean, mean, tall willowy fellow who wore heavy black framed glasses. He also took us for French. After ploughing chapter by chapter through our text book 'En Route', he would prowl up and down the aisles and between our desks armed with his size 9 gym shoe. He would then select some unfortunate lad to be quizzed on what had been gleaned from the book, then, positioning himself behind the boy – who was ordered to stand – with gym shoe poised behind his head. "Tell me, what is the French for 'the boy?' To which the unfortunate replied, "La garcon, sir". Turner raged, "How – can – you – have – a – female – boy? It is le garcon", at the same time bringing the size 9 down, in time with the staccato stops between his utterances, to the back of the boy's head. We picked up French fairly quickly in those days!"*

Music lessons were invariably amusing – for both Reynolds and me. These were held in the school hall with Bert Wheeler. Mr Osborne (Ozzie) would play piano. At our first session, Wheeler had us all stand in a group as Ozzie went into the introduction to *Jerusalem*. Blake's lyrics were displayed on large sheets attached to the wall. During the singing, Bert proceeded to walk amongst us carefully listening to each boy. He obviously wanted to ascertain who could sing, or at least carry a tune. When he got to David and me he grimaced saying, *"Get out you two, and wait for me over there in the corner"*.

At the end of the lesson he approached and told us we could not carry a tune and that we would be joining the school orchestra. Two weeks later, David and I started violin lessons with a dapper little guy called

Toby Ellen, who had been engaged by Mr Wheeler. Being in the school orchestra, or the brass band, came with certain privileges. Whereas the school interior was out-of-bounds outside of the official times, musicians were not subject to this rule. The highpoint of my time in the school orchestra was playing at the annual school Speech Day. This was held in Barrow's Public Hall, usually in the month of July, and it was a very formal event, attended by the school Governors. On one particular occasion I recall that the guest speaker was Vickers's Director, Mr W D Opher, who also presented the awards, including cups and medals for achievements in sport. Attendance at Speech Day was compulsory, however, the inducement was a day off school.

During October, 1960, I was to visit the shipyard for the second time. I was among a school party invited in to watch the launch of Britain's first nuclear powered submarine *HMS Dreadnought* by *HM The Queen*. A great deal was made in our local press about the vessel's hull being whale-shaped. I never knew the precise reason for this but I do know the feature was not continued in any of the follow-on vessels.

Further into the term, by now early 1961, we were informed the school was to undergo considerable refurbishment. During the modernisation we would be using the Drill Hall of the Territorial Army, which was opposite the school on Holker Street, for morning assembly and P.E. Also, for such as basketball, there was a fenced, yarded area – The Cage – on Dryden Street.

The **Drill Hall** on Holker Street and home of the Territorial Army. It was, for 18-months, a temporary school hall and gymnasium. *Photo: S. Henderson.*

For the next 18-months the Corporation Building Department brought our school into the 20th Century. Upon completion they left us with, *inter alia*, a state of the art gymnasium with a synthetic rubber type floor; a new school hall which had facilities – lighting etc., for use as a theatre, also inside toilets!

Later in the year dad took me into the steelworks to see the new casting plant that had been commissioned on September the 18th. This had made headlines globally as Barrow was the first works to rely on the new process, which it had pioneered, for its entire production[8]. It was my first incursion into a place I had heard so much about throughout my tender years and it was uncanny, I experienced a distinct feeling of *déjà vu.*

During this early part of the sixties the cinema was visited, on average, twice per week. I would either go alone or with friends. Films I saw that come to mind are *The Alamo* (John Wayne); *The Young Ones* (Cliff Richard); *Cleopatra* (Elizabeth Taylor); *Journey to the Centre of the Earth* (James Mason) and *G I Blues* (Elvis). For me, part of the enjoyment of seeing a good film was sharing the experience with other like-minded people. Sitting in the plush auditorium of Barrow's *Ritz cinema*, I was

An early 1900s post card depicting the new Gaiety Picturedrome (later the Essoldo) on Abbey Road. Films I recall seeing here are the Cole Porter musical, High Society also John Huston's Moby Dick. The building to the right of the cinema is the Salvation Army Citadel, in the distance and just visible is the Waverley Hotel. Note the tram lines along Abbey Road. *Frith postcard.*

Ritz Buildings on the corner of Abbey Road and Holker Street c1959
Demolished 2004. Brian Moxham *(Shadows from our past)*

Staff of the former Ritz Cinema photographed on Abbey Road in 1973. Of those known are, from left to right, Jimmy Ainsbury; the manager (centre); then right, assistant manager Mr. Fotis. *Courtesy of The Mail.*

During the summer of 1962 the Holker Street boys were to visit the Continent for the second time! In the previous year they had invaded Germany. The 1962 trip was to Brittany, northern France. On the scheduled day in July, Dave Reynolds and I walked up to the back of Palmen's house, which was on Warwick Street, where our coach awaited. In describing our transport, I would refer the reader to the opening scenes of the St Trinian's films of the 1950s, where the girls are just arriving at the start of their new school term. Our coach was just like those in the films but with St Matthew's Scouts emblazoned along each side. Once all the kit bags had been loaded, we set off on our summer holiday with Felix Palmen at the wheel. Reynolds and I sat together. I had the window seat which, I was to discover, was loose in its frame. I had to endure an irritating 'grating' sound all throughout the journey. Additionally, the seats were just like those on a Corporation service bus. There were no head rests, which told me this vehicle was not designed for inter-continental travel. Moreover, there was no air-con.

Our route south took us along the A-roads, passing through all the main towns, until, somewhere around Coventry, we joined the M1. About seven hours after leaving Barrow, we pulled onto the lorry park of the Busy Bee café, which was just north of London. Following our meal we headed into the Capital. I am not sure of our route in those pre- M25 orbital days but I remember passing by the *London Planetarium* on our way to Dover.

From Dover we took the overnight ferry to Ostend, not Calais for some unexplained reason, experiencing a somewhat rough crossing. I recall we entered Ostend harbour, just as dawn was breaking on a dreary morning.

Most of the following, very wet, day was spent in the Belgian port of Ostend and to kill time a group of us went to the cinema. The film we saw was *Barabbas*, which starred Anthony Quinn. The picture house, I recall, was unusual. Whereas at home, the floor always sloped down towards the screen, this floor sloped upwards and so we were reclining backwards looking up at the film. After this experience we continued on our journey, crossing the border into France, en route to the Normandy city of *Rouen.*

The trek across northern France seemed never ending and, as we were behind schedule, Ozzie was instructed by Felix to make some sandwiches for everyone – all forty-five of us! After stopping at a roadside boulangerie, Mr Osborne prepared a stack of treacle butties, which he duly handed around. As we continued on our way, and too busy eating my bread and treacle, I was not aware of the goings-on by those on the back seat of the coach. After about ten minutes into our journey, a car came alongside the bus signalling for Palmen to pull over. The car was an executive type from which out stepped a city-gent sort, who set about berating Palmen in a foreign tongue. It then became clear to the rest of us what had happened – we could see that stuck to the windscreen of this guy's limo, were several treacle sandwiches! Felix Palmen did not see the funny side of this prank and warned those responsible that, when we stopped for the night, retribution would be swift and terrible. We, once again, continued our journey.

On approaching the outskirts of *Rouen,* we marvelled at the Gothic architecture of the church spires and other grand buildings, also the bridges spanning the Seine. Felix had been driving now for almost two days solid so he definitely needed to rest. With the coach parked up on a space near to the river, French master Dave Teague and another of the group went around the local small hotels to arrange some accommodation for the night.

About one hour later we were organised into groups of four and shown to the digs, ours being the *Hotel des Familles,* with instructions to meet up at 10am the next morning. My group comprised Ian Campbell; Dave Reynolds; Colin Queen and myself. The next morning, upon awaking, we realised that we didn't have a watch between us and we needed to know the time so as not to be late for our rendezvous. Between us it was agreed that I would try out my schoolboy French on the char who we could hear cleaning outside in the passageway. Steeling myself I approached her, *"Excusez-moi?"* I said. *"Quelle heure est-il s'il vous plait?"* Upon hearing my question the char looked at her wrist watch and replied, *"It's half-past eight son"*, (she was obviously English). Hearing sniggers emanating from the bedroom, I felt deflated!

Following an enjoyable breakfast of omelettes, croissants and proper coffee, we set off to the coach.

After almost another full day's drive and crossing from Normandy into Brittany we, at last, pulled onto the campsite at Longchamps. It had taken us three days to get here, Felix had done well driving this old vehicle which, we must remember, had no power steering, no synchro and certainly no Sat-Nav. Our two weeks in camp turned out to be a great holiday packed with fun and laughs and, being my first time abroad, most memorable.

In October, 1962 my brother, Peter John Henderson came into the world.

It was also in 1962 that Hannah, my grandmother, left the holiday camp and took a job closer to home. The camp at Middleton was remote from public transport points and being almost 70-years old [10], was finding the travelling arduous. She had applied for, and was given, a position as chamber maid at the Grand Hotel at Grange-over-Sands. This establishment was reasonably near to Grange Railway Station. I think nanna worked at the Grand for three years and then finally retired.

Sources & Notes to Chapter Four

1 *The Wind in the Willows*, Kenneth Grahame, 1908.

2 Register of Fishing Boats (Barrow), Cumbria Archives and Local Studies Centre (Barrow).

3 *Our Barrow (Part 3), Hindpool*; Alice Leach, 1980.

4 *These Things shall be a Loftier Race*; John Addington Symonds.

5 *The Golden Treasury*; Francis Turner Palgrave, 1861.

6 *Meg Merrillies*; John Keats.

7 *The Vagabond*; Robert Louis Stevenson.

8 *Barrow Steelworks: An illustrated History*; S. Henderson and K. Royall, 2015.

9 Being beyond the reach of Miss Witham, I now feel comfortable in the use of Americanisms.

10 My grandparents were devoted believers in the Victorian work ethic. To them work was the 'be-all and end-all'. (Labor Omnia Vincit, "work conquers all"). If you weren't 'on with something' then you were loafing. Whenever we met it would be; 'Hello Stanley, what you on with'?

Note: Apropos my accounts of corporal punishment in the foregoing chapter(s), although at times maybe a little heavy handed, no kind of abuse should be inferred. It was just how things were in those days. Moreover, much light was made of it in literature and by the BBC via school comedies, on television, such as Whacko! Starring Jimmy Edwards and Billy Bunter (Gerald Campion).

The Headmaster's Study and two members of the Smokers Union are paying their dues.

Chapter Five

The Mid-Sixties

I remember the start of '63 because it was a particularly bad winter with a higher than average snowfall for our part of the country. Around this time my friendship with Dave Reynolds, outside of school, started to drift as I tended to associate more with two other local lads – both older than myself. John Baker lived just down the street from me at 34, his friend, Ian Widnall, lived on Keppel Street. Ian was a first year apprentice painter at Vickers and John was in the 5th form at Barrow Technical School [the Tech] on Howard Street. The new technical school, built in the mid-fifties by Barrow Corporation Building department to replace the original Tech on Abbey Road, also became a dual-purpose establishment. It was a state school through the day and then, in the evening, a night school being a first phase of Further Education in the town; referred to by Hindpool folk as *the College.*

The new Tech on Howard Street which opened c. 1957. The 'modern' design included a lot of glass in the east and west elevations. During the dark winter months it stood like a beacon illuminating our part of Hindpool. The building has been modified and extended over the years and in 2018 is known as College House. *Photo: S. Henderson 2018*

The Prospectus catered for such as commercial correspondence; languages; art and National Courses in naval architecture, electrical and mechanical engineering. I can recall that, on dark winter evenings, the building, which comprised a lot of glass, really lit-up our part of Hindpool.

A view of Anson and Keppel Street from the top-floor of the Tech. *Photo: M. Garforth, 1975.*

The Head Teacher was Fred Pickup. The Tech during 1963 was a very unruly establishment, possibly even to the point of being out of control! I can recall walking along Howard Street on several occasions, on my way into town, around the time of the morning break and dodging small bottles of milk being dropped from high-level windows. These were aimed at passers-by (like me).

Howard Street had suffered badly during the Blitz, along with Monk and Keppel Streets. Howard Street Technical School was built on land previously occupied by a part of these streets.

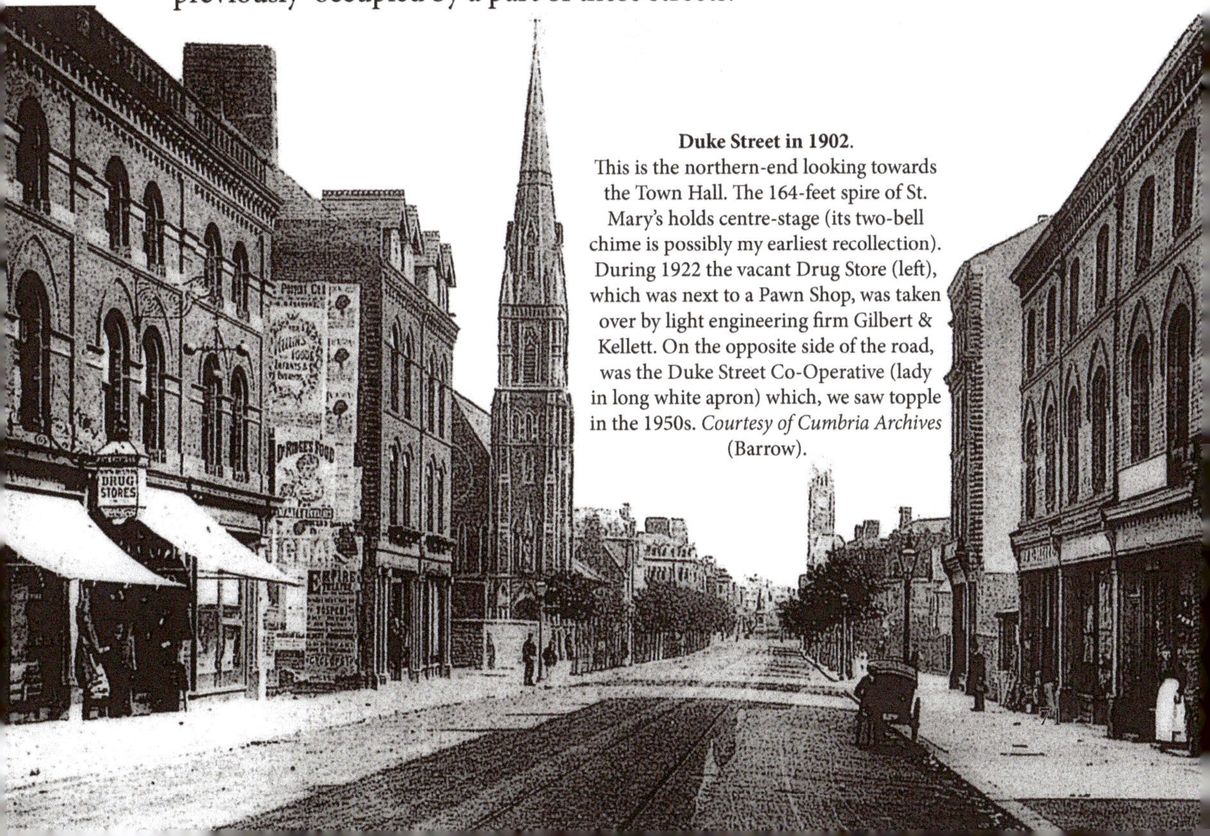

Duke Street in 1902.
This is the northern-end looking towards the Town Hall. The 164-feet spire of St. Mary's holds centre-stage (its two-bell chime is possibly my earliest recollection). During 1922 the vacant Drug Store (left), which was next to a Pawn Shop, was taken over by light engineering firm Gilbert & Kellett. On the opposite side of the road, was the Duke Street Co-Operative (lady in long white apron) which, we saw topple in the 1950s. *Courtesy of Cumbria Archives (Barrow).*

GILBERT & KELLETT LTD.

Duke Street Engineering Works
Barrow-in-Furness

ESTABLISHED 1922   Telephone : BARROW 17

Engineering work of all kinds carried out at Plant Installations throughout the District.	Jobbing and Production Work.
	Complete Machines either developed or built to customers designs.
Machining, Welding, Steelwork and Sheet-metal Work.	Prototypes or quantities as required.

John Baker left the Tech in 1963 aged 16. He secured a job as a capstan hand with Gilbert & Kellett

Across Howard Street, originally Back Duke Street North, and opposite the Tech, was the rear of the old retail units which fronted Duke Street

During 1922, one building, the Duke Street Drug Stores, had been adopted by the engineering firm Gilbert & Kellett, makers of commercial laundry and dry cleaning machinery on behalf of their parent American company. The Firm had installed capstan lathes and drilling machines on the ground floor. The noise that emanated from this large, hollow building was probably far higher than would be allowed today. Upon leaving school, in 1963, John Baker secured a position as a capstan hand with them. A few years later, by then subsumed into British Laundry Machinery Ltd, they moved to a site on Flass Lane, Roose and the Duke Street building was demolished along with the adjacent derelict properties.

Opposite the old drug stores and the pawn shop on Duke Street was the Co-operative, (later shortened to the Co-op), which was quite a large shop by the standards of the era. The demise of this building was brought about when building contractors, excavating for the new garage/forecourt for Brady's, inadvertently undermined the foundations, causing it to topple. I recall watching this, along with scores of other Hindpool children. The event provided a full afternoon's entertainment. When the site had been cleared, a single-story, prefabricated structure was hastily erected to ensure a continuity of service for local people. Additionally, the Co-op also established a new, smaller, store (Byco) on Bath Street at the corner of Vernon Street.

Howard Street after the Blitz of 8 May, 1941. This image shows the extent of the damage inflicted. Looking through the debris (left) the Ambrose Hotel on Duke Street can be seen with its roof tiles shattered. The building in the centre stood at the corner of Duke and Anson Streets. When it was eventually demolished and the site cleared, the plot became the yard of local builder Harold Mills of 51 Cook Street. It remained so for 30-years. *Courtesy of K. E. Royall.*

The Derelict Hindpool Hotel – at the left of the above terrace - viewed from the north corner of Morgan's scrapyard (currently the location of the Owl and Pussycat), during the construction of Athersmith's new depot c. 1961. Courtesy of T. Brady & Son.

I was now 14-years old and with my older friends started to venture beyond the boundaries of Hindpool. We would now regularly go 'up town', usually to the coffee bars of Franchi and Gusselli, both on Dalton Road, to listen to the latest pop records on the duke boxes. Brucciani had two outlets on Dalton Road at the time but, for some reason, we never patronised them. Dalton Road was a street of great interest to us. If ever we were at a loose end or, bored maybe, a walk along this road[1] was uplifting. There were so many individual and unique shops, all with their windows lit-up at night for the purpose of window shopping. This was before the banks, building societies and charity shops moved in. The evening was sometimes finished off with either a visit to the Sass Shop (Temperance Bar) or a portion of chips from Melville's.

The year 1963 would also see a significant and profound change for Barrow and Hindpool. The Barrow News of 18 January had reported that union officials representing the workforce of Barrow Ironworks Ltd had been told on the 16th that the works would close on the last day of March. Barrow Ironworks had been bought by the Millom Haematite Iron Company. Millom ironworks were part of the Cranliegh group who had secured a sale for £1,500.00 with the Iron and Steel Holdings and Realisation Agency. The news that broke on that day in January 1963 was devastating for the town. The ironworks was the town's oldest industry. Around 730 people would lose their jobs. The reason cited was the apparent over-production of pig iron[†††] that was building up throughout the Hindpool works. Employees started to seek alternative employment. Family friend, Norman Adams of Howe Street, who had worked at the ironworks since leaving school, decided to go for a totally new start. Later in the year he left the town for Australia as a 'ten pound Pom'.

When the ironworks finally closed, John Baker, Ian Widnall and myself started visiting the site for the purpose of doing a recce. (John's dad, Joseph, was the boss platelayer at the time. He was responsible for the upkeep

††† Pig Iron: about 17,000 tons had accumulated

of the work's internal rail network – all eleven miles of it – and he was frequently called into work through the night to deal with derailments).

Access to the works was gained through a gap in the boundary wall near to the tunnel, the underpass that connected Hindpool Road with Ironworks Road. We were surprised how easy it was to get in. There were no security arrangements at all. I remember that we visited the site, (almost) undisturbed, every night after our tea, for a week. That's how long it took us to get right around the complex, it was so large. I had a good insight into the place, having been told about the different aspects of it and the various types of plant from family and neighbours over the years. Moreover, we were taught about it while at the Jimmy's. I would bet that everyone at our school could have produced a reasonably accurate sketch of a blast furnace. I was now going to stand right next to one for the first time and I was more than excited!

Passing through the partly demolished boundary wall gave us, firstly, access to the southern end of the steelworks. We then proceeded west, crossing the British Rail main line and into the ironworks proper where we came to the two pig casting machines and the ore crushing plant. This area of the works was serviced by a narrow-gauge railway and we played about for what seemed ages, pushing the small railway cars, which were surprisingly easy to propel. There was also a hand-cranked bogey, similar to the one I first saw in the 1950s movie *Davy Crockett and the Great Locomotive Chase*. Messing around in the ironworks we were in our element. For me, in a perverse kind of way, it was better than a theme park! [Just picture me at home in my serendipity and the dream of any budding industrial archaeologist]. On a different occasion we ventured further north to the now, silent, blast furnaces. Standing at the base of these three behemoths, which were each 197-feet tall, was humbling. I had lived with their 'screaming' all of my life up to this point - and now they were silent. The whole place, in fact, was silent and much tidier and more orderly than

I had expected. The furnacemens' bothy was eerie. There were old jackets hanging up, tea mugs, newspapers and ash trays on the table – as if the men had just gone home for lunch. Nothing had been locked or cleared away. Very 'Mary Celeste', or even the spooky feeling conjured up in the airport scene in the film of Steven King's, *The Langoliers*.

Situated adjacent to furnaces 2 and 3 was the huge gas cleaning plant that I had heard so much about from family friend Major Bromley. Mr Bromley had worked on this since it was first erected around 1951, having been purchased 'second hand' from Consett steelworks in County Durham. This plant, apparently, had always been beset with operational problems and, by all accounts, had not been 'a good buy' for Barrow. To me as a 14-year old, however, it was just a huge conglomeration of twisting pipes, valves and other strange equipment, garnished in ironmongery.

The last part of the works that we explored - after taking in the 'new' blast furnace - was the Sinter Plant. [No 3 bf had recently been rebuilt from the foundations of an older model that was originally erected in 1918. It stood resplendent in its coat of red oxide primer]. Installed during 1948, the Sinter Plant - a relatively new piece of equipment - never realised its full potential at Barrow. During 1965 it was dismantled and then re-erected at the Millom works.

The Hindpool blast furnaces were identified numerically from the south. At other works these majestic, lofty, structures were assigned, as with ships, the female gender. Some works, such as at Appleby-Frodingham in Scunthorpe, named their furnaces after English queens[2]. Had the convention been adopted at Barrow we would have literally run out of queens!

On the Friday, having enjoyed almost a full week of undisturbed 'ironworks days', John and I were again accessing the southern-end of the works complex and then, as if from nowhere, we were accosted by two policemen who immediately accused us of trespassing with the intention of causing vandalism – our juvenile maraud had been arrested. The two bobbies were Sgt. Fox and Constable Brown. The upshot was that six weeks later John and myself, accompanied by our fathers, appeared before Barrow Juvenile Panel and were each fined the sum of ten shillings (50 pence), for – 'Unlawfully trespassing upon lines of railway'. We were also made to apologise to the Panel for our behaviour although, personally, I felt the week's exploration had been well worth the ten bob admission charge!

Our daily excursions into the ironworks had taken us across Hindpool Road each time. This thoroughfare, obviously in a more primitive form, existed long before the town (for many years it had a cobble-stone surface). It connected the village[3] of Barrowhead to the farms and cottages of Hindpool and Cocken. Hindpool Road, at just under one mile long, is a continuation of Strand[4], it runs north-west from the Newland Street junction and up to Walney Road. Our 1963 walk along the road, for the purpose of this exercise, starts at the Walney Road end. The Hindpool Hotel, at 140, is on this corner. During the late 19th century this was residential and it had stables to the rear. My sources tell me that from the 1930s it was a very rowdy establishment[5], not to be frequented by ladies or those of a sensitive disposition. The floor of the, very long, public bar area was just bare floorboards, covered with a sprinkling of saw-dust. This gave rise to the local saying: "see you int' saw-dust end".

Walking along past a terrace of larger type houses (numbers 122 to 138 inclusive), we come to the Wheatsheaf Inn - covered in chapter seven. This and the Hindpool Hotel are at each end of the block between Blake and Anson Street. Up until circa 1873 only the two licenced premises stood on that stretch. The terrace of houses being built some time later. (The town planners obviously having their priorities in order). Directly opposite this block is a vast walled area which, in 1963, is Sam Morgan's scrapyard. This high wall, as I recall, was caked with soot and other debris that had built up over decades. On the corner opposite to the Hindpool Hotel builders are constructing a new depot for haulage contractors, Athersmith Brothers, who are in the process of moving from their base at Symons Garage on Abbey Road. The aforementioned area [in 2018, the location of the catch-penny named Hollywood Park[6]] had originally been the extensive brick works and saw mills of local contractor, William Gradwell. There had been a dwelling in this corner of the yard directly opposite the Hindpool Hotel, most probably the home of the brickworks superintendent. The entrance to Gradwell's works was on Hindpool Road, near to the intersection with Anson Street. In his 2017 book, The Beer Houses of Barrow, Ian Wilkinson tells us that at this location once stood some old cobblestone farm cottages, two ale houses – probably the Hammer and Pincers and the Staffordshire Home - which were all demolished during the widening of Hindpool Road [pre-1873]. The area had, for a while, been referred to as 'Little Staffs'.

Continuing along past the Lower Anson Street junction we come to Clive Street and at its intersection with Hindpool Road once stood the Clive Street Chapel, also referred to as the Tin Church. It disappeared around 1930 just prior to a new rugby ground being built.

Further along and on the corner of North Road (the Low Road) is a single-story building known as *Oily Dick's,* actually the warehouse of W. B. Dick & Co., whose main premises had been at 3 Strand. They had traded in wholesale paints and other oil-based products. The warehouse has a roof of corrugated asbestos sheeting and distinct, stepped, gable ends. There was no obvious activity during the early sixties. On the opposite corner of North Rd is a little black hut, a sweet and tobacconist shop called Craven Park Stores.

Oily Dick's; a depiction of the 1960s and the original warehouse of W. B. Dick & Co by local artist Geoff Berry. This was at the junction of North Road and Hindpool Road (see Appendix 1). It had lain empty for many years, being eventually demolished in 1974 – 75.

It only seems to open intermittently such as when Barrow Rugby are playing at home or the shipyard men are going to work. The proprietor is a guy called Algy Pratt and he is a store man at the steelworks. Directly opposite is Craven Park, the home of Barrow RLFC. This had originally been a reservoir for the Flax and Jute works. For a short time it had been a greyhound track[7]. Along from the rugby stadium is an impressive building of red engineering brick. This is the British Workman's (CIU) Club, also known as the Kill-One, it had opened in 1933. Next to this stands the Corporation Bus Depot which opened in Jan 1936 (Barrow never did have a proper bus station).

The Corporation Bus Depot (Garage) on Hindpool Road. The western gable of Craven Park's grandstand is to the left of the photo. *Brian Moxham, 1983*

The Façade of the defunct, art deco, John Whinnerah Institute on the John Whinnerah Roundabout – a clever architectural illusion. *Photo: S. Henderson, 2018.*

Along from the buses and approaching Abbey Road, is a detached red, rustic-brick, building called John Whinnerah School House - the home of the caretaker of the next building. This being the John Whinnerah Institute, at the junction with Abbey Road. It also had been built (1938), on land reclaimed from the old Flax and Jute Works site and was a training facility for the Women's Institute. Later it served as the administration centre for education in the town. It was named after one-time mayor and chairman of the council's education committee. He was also a rugby enthusiast.

Retracing our steps as far as the *Kill One* and looking across the road, we see what was known as the Jute Sidings, this was where railway wagons, loaded with raw materials were parked, waiting to cross Hindpool Road into the Jute Works. At the time of our walk-by the area is a coal yard where railway wagons are unloaded, with coal weighed and bagged for such as the Co-op and Holmes's coal merchants. Next to this is the foundry

Caird's Foundry on Hindpool Road. The two tall structures are Cupola furnaces used for melting iron and steel. (They could not be used for making steel). Caird also owned the Charcoal Iron Co at Backbarrow during the 1960s; this closed down in 1968. *Courtesy of Roy Chatfield.*

of David Caird. This had previously been the Furness Foundry, established in 1884, becoming David Caird Ltd., from 1890. (It closed down in 1998). The works made such as ingot moulds and slag tubs which were supplied to steelworks all over the country. The site from 2019 has been occupied by the large retail outlets of Tesco, Iceland and Halfords.

Crossing over Abbey Road and opposite the John Whinnerah is the Custom House building. This edifice during our walk-by is a very drab, uninviting place. Originally built in 1866 as a hotel in an Italianate style, it became a government building towards the end of the 19th century and I believe it now enjoys listed status. During the 1950s, it would be passed when on our way to the gas works and we christened it the house of horrors! In stark contrast to

The Custom House building at 66 Hindpool Road As with the John Whinnerah Institute this, too, is a Grade 2-listed building. There appears to be an anomaly regarding the actual address? Although the main entrance is on Hindpool Road, the restaurant is recorded as being at 1, Abbey Road on the Companies House website. It was always my understanding that the residence of the Chief Fire Officer, at the corner of Abbey Road and Lawson Street, is 1 Abbey Road. *Photo: S. Henderson, 2018.*

its appearance today, it just had a negative effect on the observer. Pressing on and nearing the end of our walk-by, we pass a derelict Methodist chapel (built 1863), set between Laundry and Chapel Street. This had been the Hindpool Road Congregational Church, it closed in 1931. In 2018, it is occupied by Duddon Tyres Ltd. Set back from the main road is the annex to the old steam laundry which stood opposite on Hindpool Road. This establishment has, over the years, been through several incarnations. At one time being the potato warehouse of Wilf Carr.

The Congregational Church viewed from Lawson Street (rear view). It had lain empty for a number of years before becoming Woodward's Tyres after the war. In 2018, it trades as Duddon Tyres Ltd. *Photo: S. Henderson, 2018.*

Our excursion ends at Heath's Devonshire Brewery and the Devonshire public house at the corner of St Vincent Street. Opposite this is the gas works where many Hindpool folk would turn up, pushing wheel barrows and baby prams for the purpose of buying coke. I can't remember the price we paid for it but on occasion we would also purchase a drum of tar and sometimes creosote, for the shed roof. Upon arriving home with our purchases we would be filthy with dust from the coke, more so if it was windy. Happy Days!

Carr's Potato Warehouse
This building, on Laundry Street, has had several uses over the decades. Originally it had some connection with the Steam Laundry which stood opposite on Hindpool Road. Then, for years, potatoes were stored and distributed from here. When my family kept pigs I can remember collecting sacks of 'cattle potatoes' here. Potatoes had to be graded with any rejects appropriated to animal feed, they were subsequently stained with a purple dye to prohibit re-sale for human consumption. *Photo: S. Henderson, 2018.*

The gas works were as far as I ventured in those times, never having cause to go further and thus ending our walk-by. Hindpool Road, despite being a main thoroughfare, was a desolate place during the period discussed. It passed through what would, today, be called an industrial estate. I have recollections of looking along its entire length and not seeing a single vehicle, and of course, it was never a tram or bus route. Other engineering concerns which operated on Hindpool Road over the years were Messrs Stuart's Rope Manufactury (1858); Messrs Westray and Forster (ironworks & machinery); Waddington and Longbottom's Foundry and Griffith's Brass Foundry.

Heath's Devonshire Brewery from Lawson Street, it has long since ceased to perform its original function as brewing ceased in 1960. Nowadays it has multiple commercial uses, q.v. *Photo: S. Henderson.*

Hindpool Road Gas Works.
This closed down during the 1960s and the area taken over by North West Water. *Photo: N. W. Evening Mail.*

The start of 1964 saw my time occupied between walking the whippets, they needed daily road work to harden their leg muscles, feeding the poultry and watering dad's greenhouse at the small allotment we had on the Brick Work's ground. This was a large area. It was bounded on three sides by the streets, Bath, Chatsworth and Holker and on the northern side by Barrow AFC and the works of the Furness Brick and Tile Company. For some time after the Second World War it was just a large deep pond, having been a clay pit. It can be seen by reference to the aerial photo on p40. At some point during the early 1950s it was taken over by Vickers Armstrong who began using it as a tip – in fact it became referred to as 'the tip' by local people. I recall Vickers' lorries transporting load after load of empty paint tins as well as ash and cinder from the foundries. Additionally, Vickers began parking some large fabricated structures to do with their Cement Division. Slowly, as the pond reduced in size and after Vickers had withdrawn, the Brick and Tile Co began letting parcels of the reclaimed land as allotments. Allotment holders from Hindpool I remember are: Stan Bewly; Jack Crane; Artie Graham; Bob Reynolds; Ken and Ray Smith and Joe Walling. Our 'garden', immediately behind St James' Scout Hut off Chatsworth Street, became the meeting place for my friends, especially at weekends, where we would regularly tune into pirate radio station, Radio Caroline on our transistor radio. [With hormones aboil we were further cranked-up by the emerging sixties music scene]. Spending time 'up the garden' also allowed me to stay in tune with the steelworks and the perplexity of sounds emanating from this colossal place. It got that I could identify which precise piece of plant and equipment was working from the sounds I could hear. Such as the Klondyke overhead crane trundling down No 2 steel shed, or the siren that sounded to indicate to workers that the 50-ton Barcon crane was about to start moving. This fascination started, I believe, during the 1950s while playing on the swings at Piggy

Lane; I could hear the mill steam engines 'hunting' as the ingots began their journey through the cogging rolls of the rail mill.

During the 1970s, after the allotments were cleared, a large MFI store was built, this later became Argos.

Meanwhile, back at school, I was now into my mock O-levels. I had chosen five subjects and was making fairly good progress. My strongest subjects were Biology and Physics, followed by French and English. Maths remained a moot point, for reasons previously outlined.

After awakening on one particular morning, following a restless night, I came down to breakfast and announced to mother that I had decided not to stay on at school for my 'O' Levels and was going to leave at the end of the summer term. "And do what?" she snapped. I told her that I was going to apply for a job at the steelworks. Her response was to say that it would all depend on my father. My plan was to apply for a job as a Lab Assistant and, hopefully, become qualified through night school. To summarise – father was fine with my idea but insisted that whatever job I secured I would go through night school anyway.

Three months later I had an interview arranged, by the Youth Employment Service, at Barrow Steelworks. Attired in my Sunday best I reported to the works main gate and was directed, by the commissionaire, to the office of Mr Ray Carberry, the assistant labour manager. Mr Carberry's office was on the ground floor and it was like some Dickensian solicitor's chambers complete with antique furniture and time pieces that ticked away loudly (see Appendices). There was also a distinct and unusual smell about the place and of course it was scrupulously clean. Ray Carberry was a true gentleman, he immediately put me at ease telling me that my family had a good name at the works. He discounted my getting a Lab Assistant's job as the requirement was three 'O' Levels, including maths and chemistry as well as the need to be at least 16-years old, as the job entailed shift work.

He offered me instead the job of test house assistant, which was a day-shift position and within a group known as student operatives. I accepted and we shook hands. He then told me that he was duty bound to say that he couldn't guarantee long-term security of employment as the works may be closing down. I thanked him for his time and left for home.

When I arrived home dad was waiting to find how things went, so I outlined my interview also adding the coda about the possibility of the works shutting down.

"That's exactly what I was told at my interview there in 1939!" he quipped. It was at that moment I realised my life as a schoolboy was over.

Sources & Notes to Chapter Five
A History of Hindpool: James Melville, 1952.
1 I am unable to express in words just how 'alive' and vibrant Dalton Road used to be during the period discussed.
2 Ref. blast furnaces at other works, viz. – Queen Anne, Queen Bess, Queen Mary and Queen Victoria.
3 Local historian, Alice Leach, refers to Hindpool as a village. It had always been my understanding that to qualify as such, an Anglican church was necessary. Whilst I would class both Hindpool and Barrowhead as settlements, the term 'villager' does seem more appropriate than 'settler'. (Vide St.Mary's, Dalton).
4 Strand: as with Hoad at Ulverston, it was never officially 'the' Strand, per Ray Hewson, Let's all go down The Strand; (M. A. and R. Hewson, 2005)
5 Personal communication with Frank Rogan, Scotch Buildings; John Dearden and Michael Poole, Keppel Street.
6 Hollywood aka 'Sodom-by-the-Sea' where, in the 21st century, the bulk of its output is pornography.
7 Ref. Greyhounds – George Lumsden of the Wheatsheaf told me he, originally, came to the town in pursuit of this activity.
8 An account of my first day at work can be found in *Barrow Steelworks: The Open Hearth Years*

Chapter Six

People Watching

'What want and do ya good?' enquired John of his brother. 'I think I'll have another one of these, do you blame me John?' 'And I don't blame you at all Michael, I don't blame you at all', John replied.

The Queens Hotel, at the corner of Duke Street and Blake Street, was a popular Hindpool watering hole during the period covered by this book. It was also a fine, three-storey, building.

Public houses during the 1960s were not the family-friendly establishments that they later became. Pubs were the exclusive domain of the working man, a kind of retreat away from the wife and nippers! Respectable married women were seldom seen in public bars. Only at weekends, and in the singing room or smoke room, did men bring their wives or girlfriends to the local.

John Baker and I started knocking about together just prior to my leaving school. Although we were neighbours we had never previously associated – there being a two-year age gap between us. I latched on to John just after his mother had died as he seemed to be at a loose-end. His older sister, Mary, had recently married and moved away. John and I got on well together, probably because we laughed at the same things. We talked a lot, telling each other tales from our upbringing. He told me a lot about his early childhood.

Parental instructions have echoed down the years to us all at some point: 'Sit up straight! Elbows off the table! Stop picking your nose!' Like all children through the ages, I found these instructions extremely irksome. Notwithstanding, I was not prepared for what John would later disclose. 'Get your bath and then put on your gloves'. From the age of eleven some of John's male relatives (uncles) were put to bed wearing boxing gloves! I always assumed this to be a joke until years later when Joe, his father, confirmed it. I worked with Joe for two weeks in the summer of 1970 during the steelwork's stop-fortnight. This was the work's annual holiday, when essential maintenance was undertaken.

The public bar of the Queens became part of our regular week-day routine. We would go in for an hour between 7.30 and 8.30pm. and, being ensconced in a corner, we wouldn't be noticed as the bar was so large. (As a comparison it was on a par, size-wise, with the bar of the Duke of Edinburgh Hotel on Abbey Road).

The Rodgers family of Lyon Street kept pigs at Ormsgill in the area known to locals as the *Dingle*. They rented their holding from the Furness Brick & Tile Company. Michael (Mick) worked as a blacksmith's striker at the steelworks. Johnny was a crane driver in the assembly shed at the shipyard. From about 8pm, on most evenings, after they had 'done-up' at the piggery, they would go into the bar of the Queen's Hotel.

The Queens had been an actual hotel back in the old days. It occupied a prominent position with, at one time, its own tram-stop on Duke Street. It had twelve rooms on two floors. There was also a coach house to the rear, which incorporated a hayloft. This facility was accessed from Howard Street. The Queens had three entrances. The main entrance, on Duke Street, was up two stone steps from the pavement. Once inside the entrance, the public bar was on the left, a reception lounge was to the right. The hotel entrance was by way of a long corridor with a black and white chequered tiled floor. The hotel reception was a sliding window to the left and halfway along the corridor. At the end of this corridor was a wide stairway leading to all rooms. There was also an entrance to the large public bar on Blake Street, which was later bricked-up. Another entrance, to a singing room, was also on Blake Street and near to the corner with Howard Street. All the interior doors were padded and upholstered with a black imitation leather material attached with a series of padded buttons. This finish gave a plush appearance. Being a Thompson house the place had the characteristic *beery* odour in common with others of the Thompson group. All pubs in the town that were supplied by local brewers had their own distinctive smells, probably because of the use of wooden barrels. (This odour disappeared when the local brewers were bought-out by the large brewing concerns1 when metal casks replaced the wooden barrels and refrigeration became the norm). The publican during the 1960s was a Lenny Baynes. Pub landlords were not chummy in those days. They gave an air of being middle class. They were usually formally attired (suited) and carried an air of respectability. Publicans also tended to socialise with others of their ilk, usually through their own trade association – the Licenced Victuallers - or the local Round Table.*

James Thompson had no official brewery in Barrow. Up until 1929 his ales came from Chorley. After this date he brewed at Heath's Devonshire Brewery on Hindpool Road then, from 1932, at the Hartley brewery in Ulverston. In 1966 the Thompson pub estate (48 licenced premises) and the Albert Street bottling plant was sold to Whitbread.

On one particular occasion when John and I went into the Queen's bar we sat near to the Rodgers brothers. What amused us both was that these two Irishmen were absolute conversational bores! They would just sit sipping their beer in absolute silence! Then, when one of them (Johnny

* Large concerns: Bass-Charrington; Hammond; Ind Coope and Whitbread.
(To name a few.)

for instance) had drained his glass he would stand up and announce, "Well Michael I think I will get myself another one of these, do you blame me Michael?" to which Michael would reply, "And I don't blame you John, I don't blame you at all". It would then revert back to silence until either one had again emptied his glass, after which we would hear the same old. These two men were totally oblivious to the fact that the two skitty teenagers sitting opposite, were mocking their antics! (I mean, what was this 'blame' thing they kept going on about? It made no sense!).

Also, around eight-thirty, more locals would appear. Joe and Judy Walling also lived on Lyon Street. Joe was a pigeon fancier and his loft was on the Brickwork's allotments near to where the Argos Store is in 2024. Judy was a very placid boxer bitch. Joe would order his pint of mild and then teem around a third of it into one of the large glass ashtrays that were found on the tables around the room. Placing it on the floor under his table, Judy would lap it up. This would be the routine until Joe had finished his fourth pint. The pair would then stagger out of the bar, making their way back home. Also, about this time, Sam McCready appeared. Sam always turned out smart, usually in a light grey suit but contrasted by a flecked workman's flat cap. He was a big fellow and he liked his best bitter (Thompson's was a potent brew. The downside was that it had a short shelf-life, probably because of the type of yeast used in the brewing process. When the large brewers started making *export* beers in later years they somehow gained a longer life). At weekends Sam was a 20 pint man! He had lived for many years in the Scotch Buildings. When they were demolished during the late 1950s, he moved to the Ormsgill council estate. Because of the distance Sam bought himself a carrier bike, which he would park this in the ginnel at the side of the pub. There was one occasion that I recall where John and I were leaving via the Duke Street door en route to the Wheatsheaf, when we noticed that some disgusting *animal* had left Sam a nasty surprise! Perched on the leather saddle of his bicycle was a huge, megalithic *jobbie*! A soiled hanky on the ground nearby proved its human provenance. We immediately made ourselves scarce for fear of being blamed (there's that word again!).

Like Sam McCready, Owen Daley was also a very big man. He lived on Walney Road with his brothers, Tommy (Tot); Richard (Dick) and sister Eileen (Gertie). He had worked at the Slag Reduction Works on Ormsgill Lane but was now retired. He came to the Wheatsheaf on Hindpool Road every night around 6pm. He, too, came on a carrier bike which he would wheel home. It was obvious that the purpose of these bicycles was to assist in getting home without appearing too drunk. Whenever you asked Owen how he was the reply always came back the same. 'Nicely', followed by a loud burp that came out as BEW! Owen was not the most visually appealing of men. He had a very large tongue, which kept darting in and out of his mouth, almost like a reptile. His sister Gertie had the same tic! You could always identify what his most recent meal had been from the stains and gravy scabs down the front of his waistcoat. He was unique in that he always reckoned his pension in terms of pints of beer! Beer was his number one priority. Years later, after arriving home from the pub, he had taken his dog out before retiring. A speeding car on Walney Road clipped Owen, knocking him down. Sadly he never recovered. After Owen's funeral, dozens of unopened wage packets were found under his bed!

Ken and Ray Smith also lived in Lyon Street. Their front door was directly opposite that of the Rodgers family. Ken was a joiner and Ray had been a merchant seaman but during the sixties was retired. He was considered wealthy (for those days). The brothers spent most of their leisure time on their allotment, which was adjacent to Joe Walling's. What was unique about the pair was that on their allotment they had an old-style fire engine they had bought from the local fire brigade. They had constructed a large garage to house the vehicle which had been reported on in the Evening

Mail, Barrow's local newspaper at the time. Additionally, scores of children would turn up to watch Ken and Ray clean and then operate the great extending ladder. I believe their intention was to show the vintage machine at steam rallies and country fairs.

Ray Smith occasionally called into the Wheatsheaf. He was an interesting character, mainly because of his time spent abroad in the MN. He was, however, prone to romancing and so there was a limit to how long one could endure his company.

There was one dear old lady in our street with whom I must conclude this chapter. Mary Conway lived near to the top of Hood Street (49) during the 1950s. She lived alone, apart from her feline companions. No one seemed to know anything about her as she was a very private individual. Looking back I feel that she had been either a school teacher or bank clerk maybe? She was always dressed the same, a demure knee-length pleated skirt, blouse and cardigan. She devoted her time to caring for her pets - about four or five exotic cats. One in particular was called *Bum-Bum*. It wore a disc attached to its collar displaying this. *Bum-bum* was possibly Persian. If memory serves, there was also one called *Tang-Tang* which had extremely long legs. *Bum-Bum* would frequently go AWOL and Miss Conway would go in search of it. Quite often, while playing in the street with friends, Mary would approach us and ask – "have you seen my *Bum-Bum*?"

Chapter Seven

The Wheatsheaf Inn

The *Wheatsheaf Inn* and the *Hindpool Hotel* [both on Hindpool Road] stood at each end of the terrace between Blake and Anson Streets. The interposed houses being built later.

Because the *Wheatsheaf* looms large in my Hindpool story I deemed it essential for it to have its own chapter. During the days when it was my local I was not aware that it had in fact been two beer houses made into one. Upon discovering this it became clear why it had two doors, on Anson Street, right next to each other and each with its own address, i.e. 2 and 4 Lower Anson Street.

Built in 1862, it was first licensed to serve beer in February, 1873 and then granted a wine licence a year later. This was in the name of first licensee, Thomas Lambert, who had ran the *Old House at Home* for nine years previously.

It was offered for sale in October 1878 at a property auction held at the Bull Hotel on Paxton Street, Barrow, with the reserve price set at £475. In the event it was 'knocked down' to one Edwin Dawson of Burton-on-Trent for £820. The high price was commented on in the local press. (According to Alice Leach in *The Religious of the Sacred Heart of Mary* the building was owned at one point by a Mr Sutton (Daniel?) who was one of the overseers on the Bessemer Plant at the Steelworks. He apparently rode to work on a black horse with a solid silver harness). Sutton also owned two other town centre pubs. The Inn was acquired by the Truman brewery, for an undisclosed amount, during 1898 with new tenant, Mrs Sarah Cranshaw, taking up residence on 9th July. An earlier landlord, Thomas While, had hosted a Christmas party for 40 old friends on December 27th, 1881 which was described as an enjoyable evening. As part of the get-together several toasts were made during the evening to the health of Queen Victoria and other members of the Royal Family. Toasts of 'good prosperity' were also bestowed on the British Army and Naval Forces. The evening was brought to a close with a sing-along.

An artist's impression of the co-existence of **The Old House at Home** with the **Wheatsheaf** around 1900. This area of Hindpool, at one time, had been known as 'Little Staffs'. *Courtesy of Geoffrey Berry 2018*

Several well-known songs of the day were completed including: *Willie Brewed a Peck of Maut; Old Mulberry Bush; Here Upon Guard I Am; The Charge of the Light Brigade* and *Going Home with Willie.* The evening concluded with the customary chorus of the National Anthem.

The *Wheatsheaf* had been subject to considerable structural alterations and rebuilding during 1929. The closure of the adjacent *Old House at Home* was instrumental in the costly development of the Inn. The new facilities made available at the *Wheatsheaf* warranted the old beer house suitable to hold a full spirits licence. More so than several of the town's older licenced premises.

The Old House at Home ceased trading at some point in 1927. Its licence ran until 1929, when it lapsed. This allowed the *Wheatsheaf* to extend into the vacant premises. The outgoing landlord, John Henry Ridge, taking over the running of the *Ambrose Hotel* on Duke Street.

In 1931 the Sheaf became the first in the history of the town to be granted a licence to host live music[2]. This was in the name of Ernest Whittaker who had the pub from 1923 up until 1936. From 1936 until 1938 the landlord was one Joseph Lightbowm.

The Wheatsheaf was, for over half a century, the regular haunt of iron and steelworkers, also a second home to many Barrow RLFC players and supporters,

From the end of the Second World War the place became, arguably, the most popular destination in the town. Folk would queue outside on a Sunday lunchtime to imbibe its quality beers and ribald humour, the aim being to secure a seat in the singing room where pianist-entertainer Vic Dempsey, drummer Jimmy Kitchen and harmonica player Larry Moore (Barrow's Larry Adler) would knock 'em dead! In these times the *Wheatsheaf* attracted the cream of the town's local talent. Names like key board player Frank Vicary; Joey Dickinson; Ged Coulter; George Philips; Sheila

Wheatsheaf singing room (occasion unknown) during the mid-1950s. From left to right are: compere Vic Dempsey; drummer Jimmy Kitchen; Larry Moore (Harmonica); Tommy Atkinson and Stan Henderson. *Photo D. Crabtree.*

Carter. Even Billy West, the town's Al Jolson, made appearances. Occasionally some of the acts appearing at the town's 99 Club during the 1960s (including compere Tommy Halfpenny) would make an appearance. Two names that come to mind are Millie Small (*My Boy Lollipop*, 1964) and Irish tenor, Josef Locke, who, on one occasion stayed in a caravan across Hindpool Road in Sam Morgan's scrap yard. One of the most popular local figures during the 1960s was carouser Derek Pearson (Peo).

Derek, a pocket-tenor for many years in local amateur productions, restricted his singing to the bar area – which would bounce during his lusty renditions of Rodgers and Hammerstein classics, usually with alternative lyrics! Peo would nearly always be in the company of his employer, local butcher, John Fisher.

The copper-topped bar of the Wheatsheaf during the 1990s, by which time it had become cluttered with 'novelty' beers. It did, however, retain its very homely atmosphere. *Courtesy of The Mail.*

ING OF THE CANS.

WHEATSHEAF

Looking west along Hindpool Road circa 1983, the Wheatsheaf is on the right. To the left, behind the hoarding, are the offices of William Gradwell's works. The melting shop of the Continuous Casting Plant is in the distance. *D. Walmsley.*

Mine Hosts, from sometime during 1939, were Gladys and George (Jock) Lumsden who ran the business with mother-in-law Mrs (Ma) Ritson and her daughter Agnes. (No one outside of the family was allowed behind the bar). During peak times of business Ma could be heard to call out – *'wheel 'em in'*. The waitress at weekends, when the singing room was open, was Marjorie Moore (Barrow's one-time Mayoress, being the daughter of Mayor Mrs Winn). Marjorie was unbelievable! She could carry a tray of 10 or 12 pints with one hand and could also remember every drinks order without having to write them down.

Perhaps the most well-known post war character was *'enfant terrible'* Eric Finlay aka the Fin. Eric was a wit known for his racy monologues – which he would deliver with gusto on most Saturday nights. When sufficiently primed he would start off the evening with, either -

Inn-Keeper, inn-keeper, fill my men's tankards, water my horses and throw another log cabin on the fire. Or,

Here we sit in mortal bliss, down the Wheatsheaf, on the . . . .'
And we were off to the races!

Among the bar regulars during the 1960s were: Freddy Akred; Brian Bell; Cosh Caulfield; Charlie Cole; Dennis Chelton; Jim and Les Cresswell; Joe Douglas (Joe Douglas lived at 11a Anson Street. It was a corner house. He always maintained it had been a beer house years earlier, known as Star of Tivoli. This couldn't be verified); Mick Ducie; Len Finlay; Tommy Grizedale; Alfie Hadwin; Colin Haythorne; Ivor Kelland; Bobby Little; Geoff and Ray McGuire; Bill Monk; Roger Moffatt; Neville Potts; Alan Thompson aka the Duff; Bill Vickers; Bill Wookey; and Amos 'Yorkie' Whitehead. Yours truly and John Baker (the piglets). Occupying the bar extension [TV end], were: John Bell; Cliff Brown; Bill 'Napper' Cooksey; Billy and Owen Daley; the Ducie twins (Ged and Jimmy); Harry Goodwin; Jim McGlennon and Ronny Warriner.

One of the many crazy games the locals involved themselves in was the *Eating Competition*. The one that I witnessed was a fish & chip eating contest between Amos Whitehead and Ike Wade - who had come over from the *Queens Hotel*. Both of these characters were big guys, with also big appetites. The winner on this particular occasion was Amos who ate seven fish suppers! On another occasion Amos won a tripe eating competition – where he consumed a bucket full of the stuff.

An indication as to the quality of the beer (the bitter was known widely as jungle-juice), was the absence of keg beers (Other pubs in these days offered such as *Whitbread Tankard, Watney's Red Barrel and Draught Guinness* – Lager was only available in bottles). The only draught brews on offer down the 'Sheaf were *Truman's mild or best-bitter* (Jock never stocked ordinary bitter). He knew his customer base, the ale was like nectar and was what the punters (who were constantly being reminded by prominent posters to 'get on the trail of the hoppiest-ale') wanted. The best bitter in this pub had a certain quality, it was moreish?... nay, it was bloody addictive! I had heard it said, on more than one occasion, that Jock used to add something to it! This was evidenced by the fact that the ale in the town's other Truman houses, tasted slightly different.

Truman's Brewery was originally established in London during the 17th century. It was probably the oldest then later the largest brewery in the world. In 1873, it purchased Philip's Brewery in Buton-on-Trent. The Truman beers supplied to the Barrow pub estate were brewed in Burton.

The company's fortunes took a downturn when, during the 1960s, it had to come to terms with the rise of draught lager as well as competition from cheap imports. Truman's brewery was closed in 1989.

Other Truman houses (Truman Hanbury & Buxton Ltd) in Barrow were; *The Britannia*, Church Street; the *Derby Hotel*, Dalton Road the *Trevelyan* on Dalkeith St and the *White House Hotel* on Abbey Road.

As well as being a house of fun, the pub also had a negative side. It had been the cause of some unhappy marriages and break-ups. Thursday, for many years in Barrow, was pay-day for the majority of men who were on weekly pay and the first port of call, for some, after finishing work at 5pm, was the bar of the 'Sheaf. I have memories of tearful women outside of the entrance, asking patrons to see if their 'Harry' was in the bar. They obviously needed some house-keeping money to buy food. On the rare occasion I have seen a wife walk into the bar and deposit a cooked meal over some drunken husband's head. Then, on lunchtimes at weekends, some of the local gardeners would wait outside selling fresh-cut flowers, peace offerings for hapless husbands to take home!

Along with John Baker and Stewart McCorquodale, I followed the *Wheatsheaf* from 1965 to 1970. We would usually go in at around 7pm and stay till about 10pm, every day. Because, at first, we were under-age Jock insisted we stay in a corner and keep a low profile. It didn't take long for us to be accepted by the regulars and being asked if we wanted Jacks for Don, which apart from the odd game of Cribbage, was the only card game played. Sometimes we would break our routine and visit the *Furness Hotel*, on Bath Street. During the 1950s and early 60s the Landlord was Bill Barker. The Furness was a Thompson House and the beer was not as good as Truman's. Nevertheless it was a good house with a vibrant following. For a while, on Thursday nights during 1965, we would go upstairs into the function room where Billy Barker Jnr and his band would be rehearsing. I recall having some enjoyable sessions, along with John Baker, John Begley and Mike Boardley; listening to Billy and the Barnstormers.

During the Lumsden's tenure the *Wheatsheaf* was a very lucrative concern. This was despite not having a food offering; loud music; trendy drinks nor indeed any gimmicks. Never before had there been such a coming together of wit, talent and personalities. The place could have easily been the last bastion of the Anacreontic Society – in its celebration of wine, women and song[‡‡‡].

(In the mid-1970s the Lumsdens retired (for some reason, avoiding a farewell buffet that had been laid on). Bill Taylor, who had been landlord of the *Abbey Tavern*, took over. Over the next decade or so the place went into a gradual decline. Sometime during 1992 an enthusiastic Mike Fallon, who together with his wife, became proprietors. They undertook some interior modifications and once again the pub became a popular draw). What a shame then, that one of the town's most popular watering holes was closed down – along with several other town centre inns and, during 2016 – 17, renovated and made into luxury apartments.

NB: An edited version of the above chapter, compiled in collaboration with Brian Moore, appeared in Barrow's The Mail during August, 2017.

Sources & Notes to Chapter Seven

1 The Register of Electors from 1938 et seq, gives the Inn's address as 121 Hindpool Road. Following the introduction of Post Codes in the 1970s, the address once again became Anson Street.
2 Paraphrased from, and with acknowledgements to, The Beer Houses of Barrow-in-Furness by Alan Wilkinson, 2017.

‡‡‡ Years later, by which time I had increased my circle of contacts; it came to my attention, via ex-servicemen and Merchant Navy bods, that the Wheatsheaf had been spoken about in bars and dives around the globe. The concensus being that the two components that constitute a 'good house' are good beer and good company. Was there ever such a house the length and breadth of Merry England?

Epilogue

In coming to the end of my journey it is hoped I have added to the rich tapestry that is history. The Hindpool story is like a patchwork quilt made from fragments or patches of time, which are all different in size, shape and pattern.

The district, post millennium, is different to the era covered in my account. It would be easy for me to say that Hindpool is not as good as when I lived there. But no, I cannot say that, all I can say is that it is very different – it has changed. I was one of the many who registered their dismay at the demolishing of St James' Junior School around 20-years ago, to be replaced with a prefabricated building. However, having been afforded the privilege of my own guided tour of the new school by the then Head Teacher, Angela Rawlinson* in September, 2018, I was most impressed. I witnessed first-hand a commitment and enthusiasm that inspires.

The school moves forwards whilst retaining a proud link to its past. The motto *Care, Share and Respect* is still relevant.

Some of Hindpool's ' Patches',
Courtesy of the late Alice Leach.

* Angela has since retired and the present Head Teacher is Jacqueline Rushton

Appendix One

Holker Street School

Holker Old Boys Association

Childhood Health

Barrow AFC

Henry Thompson - Last Ritz Organist

Miscellaneous

The Bell Family

Holker County Secondary School

Teaching Staff (1960 – 64)

Mr G Vaughan, Head Teacher
Mr A. Wheeler, Assistant Head, Music, Science Subjects
Mr J Ashworth, Languages
Mr D Blackhurst, Mechanics
Mr E Diamond, Nautical Studies
Mr Downing, History, Crafts
Mr E Fisher, Science Subjects
Mr R Helm, PE, Games
Mr E Johnson, RI, English
Tex Kendall?
Mr F Knott, Woodwork
Mr G Osborne, Horticulture, Music
Mr E Page, Art
Mr F Palmen, Mathematics
Mr P Patterson, Woodwork
Mr B Probert, Geography
Mr Purvis, French
Mr Rudlinger, Technical Drawing
Mrs Slater, History
Mr Scott, Metalwork
Mr D Teague, French
Mr E Stott, Metalwork, Mechanical Engineering
Mrs Vickerstaff, School Secretary

Class of '60 (Form 1A)

Mike Batty
Paul Burns
Ian Campbell
Andy Coward
Charlie Davies
Roger Brill-Edwards
Ray Farish
Keith Finlay
Alex Gaydon
Dick Hammond
Stan Henderson
Mr Hodgson
Ray Henry
James Higgins
? Huddleston
Charlie Kells aka Karl Heinz-Kells
David Keen
David Kinnell
Colin Leak
Doug Martin
Neil McKinnon
D.McLelland
Ian McCulloch
Brian Mulholland
Jeff Morgan
Geoff Moss
Ray Oakley
John O'Neil
Steve Murray
David Pass
Dave Peart
R. Pearce
Michael Rennie
Dave Reynolds
David C. Reynolds
Derek Shields
Ray Searle
Geoff Simm
Tony Simpson
Terry Swarbrick
Barry Stevens
John Stevens
Roly West
Ron Windward
David Wright

'Where God's command,
mere mortals must obey.'

Holker

Teachers at the school during the 1960s tended to be, generally, of two types. There were those who had taken the academic route through university and up to degree level. Probably Ashworth; Fisher; Downing; Page; Palmen; Slater and Teague. Then the artisan types who had aspired to teaching from the ranks of tradesmen, attaining City & Guilds qualifications. These tended to focus on the vocational subjects. I found that whilst, as with Mr. Scott, you could take the man out of tin-bashing, you couldn't take tin-bashing out of the man.

Pupils were streamed according to ability and natural bent. The first year was divided into the traditional A, B and C streams. Then, after pupils had been assessed, the second year became A; T1, T2 and H (T for technical, H for horticultural also nautical studies).

Only the A stream took languages; T and H being chiefly vocational. The school garden was on Hawcoat Lane opposite its junction with Oxford Street. H stream students would plan, then work and manage the garden through to harvest (I don't know what became of the garden produce). Felix Palmen was a different person when on holiday. In school, however, he could be a formidable adversary.

Class 3T2 at Christmas 1962. This photo was taken in the school yard near to the bike sheds (Milton St end). Among those known are: (left to right) Mr E.Stott; Roy Tinning; George Bull, unknown, Frank Marshall; Ray Searle; unknown; Jimmy Cooksey.

Holker Old Boys

(Ref. Chapter 3)

Despite now being located at Hawcoat, the Holker Old Boys Association started in Hindpool. The club came about following a game of cricket played at Furness Abbey one balmy June evening in 1936 where a suggestion was turned into reality via the enthusiasm of a core of young sportsmen. Mr. K. W. [Boss] Sawrey, a very keen supporter of local sport, became President; Mr. W. [Cherry] Edmondson, Chairman and Mr. W. Livingston [Livvy] became Secretary. The club, up until 1941, was administered from a private address on Holker Street. During this year, however, the Association sought a proper clubhouse and were permitted to utilize a premises that had been handicraft rooms of Holker Street School. The building, on Blake Street, but also accessed from Bath Street, allowed the Association to develop the social side of the club's activities. From 1942 dances, concert reviews, snooker and table tennis were just some of the activities available to members. It was at one of these events that my parents first met. My father, at the time, played in the Old Boys Senior A football team (1942 – 43 season).

Old Boys go Professional.

The North Western Evening Mail of 17th November, 1945 gave a clear picture of the wealth of talent at the Holker Club. It noted: Sixteen Holker Old Boys have signed professional forms, with Barrow, including - Con McFarland; Wilf Livingston and Bill Phillipson. Eight signed with Netherfield F.C. – George Baxter; George Biggs; Stan Henderson; Dougie Hickton; Bill Richardson; Ken Richardson; Les Wood and Jack Willman.

In 1963 the author joined the club as a social member where it is recalled we played darts, snooker also enjoying the comfort of the lounge. We also had lessons in gymnastics from Chick Parsons. Other committee men I recall are Alec Finch; Johnny Staunton and Vic Cresswell.

The original clubhouse on Bath Street, this had been the Handicraft Rooms of Holker Street School. *Photo S. Henderson, 2018.*

During 1973 Old Boys left the Bath Street building and moved to the more bijou environs of Hawcoat and into a brand new clubhouse off Rakesmoore Lane. An addition to the social side was the obtaining of a drinks licence. Members could bring their wives and girlfriends for a proper night out (I think that the strongest drink I ever had in the old premises was Oxo!)

Childhood Health

(Ref. Chapter 3)

Substantial advances in public health methods had occurred during the first half of the twentieth century, advances that would have been unthinkable in the latter part of the nineteenth. These, together with improved sanitation, resulted in a marked decline in infectious diseases. Notwithstanding, when I compare my observations of schooldays during the 1950s to those of the 21st century, I realize that there were still those, in my era, who were beset with chronic conditions. At St James' Junior School I recall two wearing leg-irons due to Polio. The main affliction at the time appeared to be concerning eyes. Several in my class wore National Health Service spectacles, usually with a plaster covering one lens. There were some with a 'turn' in their eye. 'Lazy' eyes were common as were mattery eyes, denoting some form of infection. These children also tended to be on the puny side and were usually from a dysfunctional or disadvantaged home. Catarrh was also a common thing, with many children having snotty noses. Cruelly, they were labelled - Silver Sleeves or Green Sleeves. The point in writing this piece about children's health and well-being is to comment on the marked improvement seen in just 25-years while taking my own children to school during the early 1980s. I could see the quantum leap made within a generation. As I write this, however, the pendulum seems to have swung the other way. Concerns are being expressed about childhood obesity as the effects of affluence suggest we are now "killing our kids with kindness".

My family did not enjoy the luxury of a bathroom until 1954 [we used an outside toilet up until 1976], prior to this we would go to the Public Wash Baths on Abbey Road once a week. Things were improving through the 1960s although our fathers, however, were still ignorantly working away with stuff like asbestos in the local industries.

Lower Hindpool

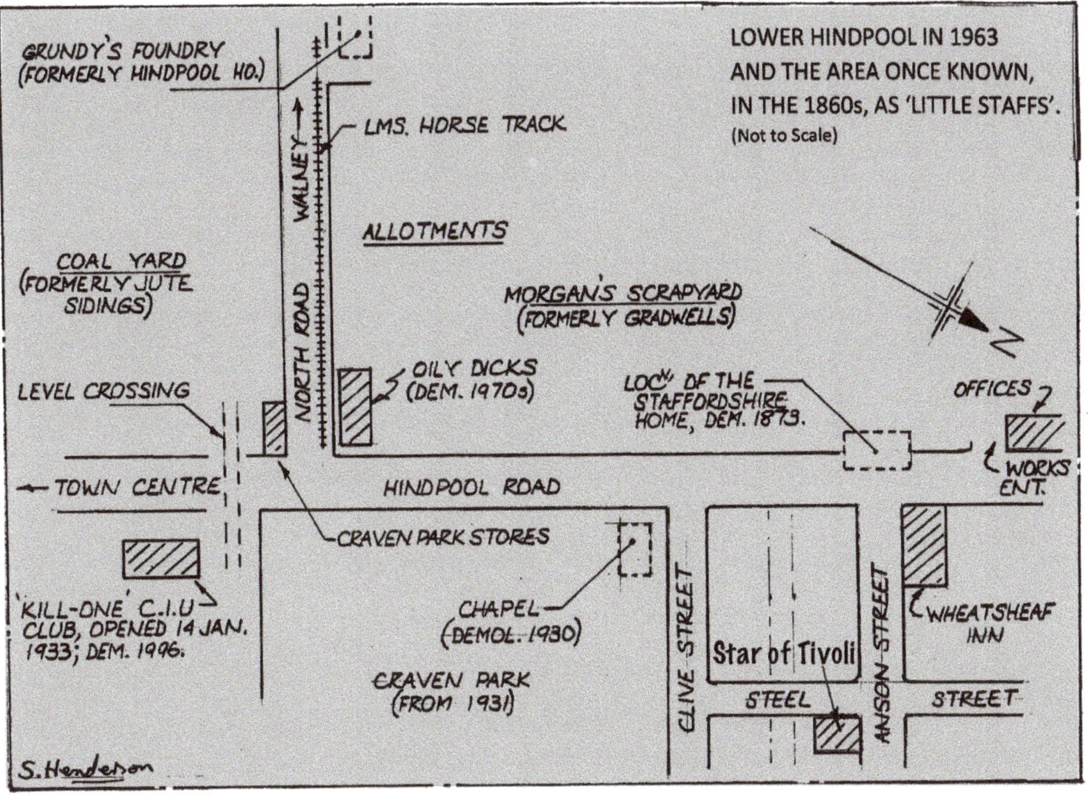

Diagram of Lower Hindpool and the area once referred to as Little Staffs. S.Henderson.

A feature of North Road during the period was the LMS Horse Track (this can be seen in the diagram above and also on the photo of Grundy's Foundry). Goods, including the bulk of Dick's products, came into the town by rail, being deposited at a goods depot - a building at the end of Ferry Road - adjacent to Burt Boulton's timber yard. During the 1920s these goods were distributed by horse and cart. From the railway bridge and up to Hindpool Road, the gradient was steep, so to assist the horses a cobble-stone track was lain. At the top of the track and outside of Dick's warehouse was a cast iron crane that swung away from the building for unloading the merchandise. Per J. Stockton.

Barrow AFC

(Ref: Mid-Sixties)

Although preferring football played with the oval ball, John Baker and I enjoyed the 1965/66 & 66/67 seasons supporting the Ziggers at Holker Street.

This came about because we had started frequenting the supporter's club – known as the Soccer Bar. This was situated under the [wooden] grandstand and accessed from Devonshire Road, later becoming Wilkie Road. The Soccer Bar attracted several Hindpool characters as well as employees of the Hoop Works. One fellow in particular that I recall, who held us spellbound with tales of his days among the South Sea Islands, was Ernie Hilton. Like the subjects in the painting by John Everett Millais, '*The Boyhood of Raleigh*', we would listen enraptured. Mr. Hilton lived on Parker Street.

Speedway queue

The entrance to Barrow AFC on Wilkie Road, The Wilkie Road elevation has since been rebuilt with concrete blocks, its stark appearance no longer projects the original character of the club. *Courtesy of The Mail*

It was not long before we started attending the home matches which, in those days, were played on Saturday afternoons. These were the Don McEvoy days and goal-keeper Fred Else had recently been signed. Else had previously played for Preston North End and another club, he became very popular with the local supporters. Fred settled in Barrow after his professional days were over. Other prominent names recalled are Bobby Knox; Mick Hartland and Brian Arrowsmith.

Perhaps Hindpool's greatest football supporter was William (Billy) Hackett. Billy was a simpleton, he was a very well-known and popular local character during the 1950s and 60s. He was best known for the exhortation, *"Come on Barra"*, which could be heard throughout the streets any day of the week. Bill also had a preoccupation with chewing gum. *"Got any chuddy mate?"* Would be what you could expect to be greeted with whenever you encountered him. Although having connections with an address on Melbourne Street, he lodged with the Greer family who ran a grocer's shop in Anson Street, opposite the police houses.

John Baker and I enjoyed some good football at Holker Street and Barrow had just gained promotion to the Third Division.

Henry Thompson, Last Ritz organist
(Ref: Mid-Sixties)

Henry Thompson, who lived on Biggar Bank, Walney Island, was the manager of the Research Laboratory at Barrow Steelworks during the time I worked there in the mid-sixties. An earlier memory, however, is from the former Ritz cinema where, for quite a few years, he was a regular feature. The news cutting, on the next page, is from the North Western Evening Mail of 24 April, 2002 and is a brief obituary. The article refers to the cinema's organ as being a Wurlitzer, I can only ever recall the organ at the Ritz being a Compton[§§§].

Saturday mornings at the ABC Minors is an abiding memory. The programme would start at 10am with Henry at the organ rising up to stage level and playing the ABC Minor's song, to which upwards of, about, 800 Barrow children would all join in; the place would literally erupt!

Children of today have more materially but nothing compared with the fellowship of our Saturday shows at the Ritz. The atmosphere was electric!

The ABC Minor's Song (tune: *Blaze away*)

'We are the boys and girls well known as,
Minors of the ABC. .
And every Saturday all line-up to see the
films we like and shout aloud with glee,
We like to laugh and have our sing-song,
Such a happy crowd are we – ee,
We're all pals together,
We're Minors of the ABC.'

§§§ Compton organs were the most prevalent theatre organs throughout the UK. They were a very vesatile instrument. They could reproduce the chimes of Big Ben; the bells of St Martins-in-the-field also the great bell carillons.

The Coliseum, which was diagonally opposite the Ritz on Abbey Road, made an attempt to copy the ABC Minors format in the 1950s. (I think I attended once). We were given badges stating – *'I'm a Colly Mickey Mouse'*.

FOND MEMORIES: Henry Thompson at the organ with his friend, Ronnie Bosson, left

Death of former cinema organist

Extract from the North Western Evening Mail of 24 April, 2002 reporting the death of Ritz organist, Henry Thompson.

Miscellaneous

A view of 'Hindpool Town Hall' being enjoyed from the swing park at Piggy Lane, 1980s.
Courtesy of Barrow-in-Furness in old photos, *Bri Mc.*

The Wheatsheaf Serviced Apartments of Blake-Henderson Ltd in 2018 viewed from Hollywood Park

The Queen's Hotel which stood at the corner of Duke Street and Blake Street; built: 1867, dem 2005. This had been residential with 12 bedroom also stables and a coach house to the rear. *D. Gardner.* (when playing Hid and Seek as a youngster I would sometimes hide in the roof-space of the coach house, needless to say I was seldom found).

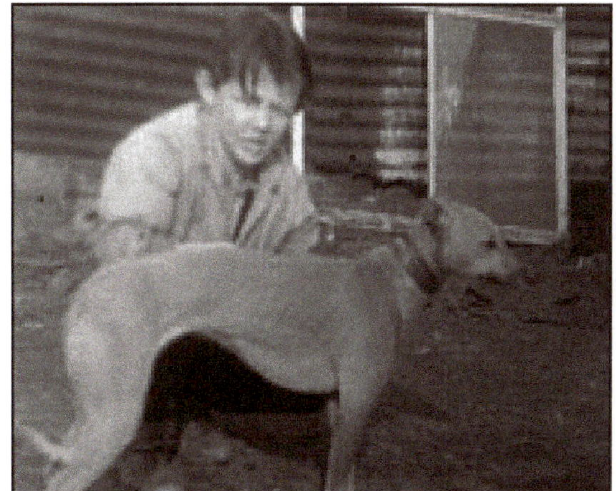

The Author at the allotment in 1961 with one of the whippets

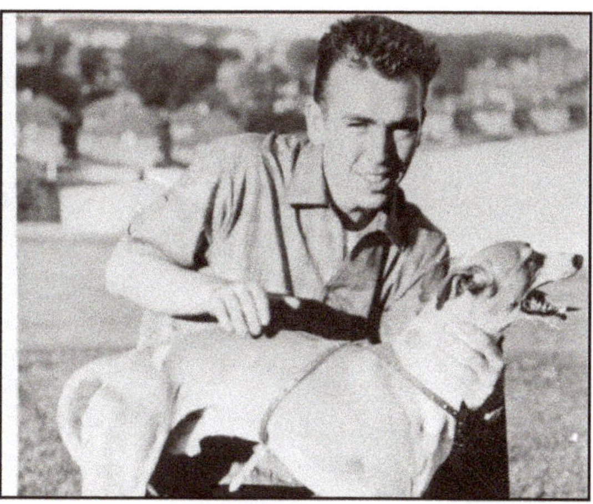

Albert Brennan of Ormsgill with *Clipper,* winner of the West Cumberland Handicap at Whitehaven, 1963. *Brennan family photos.*

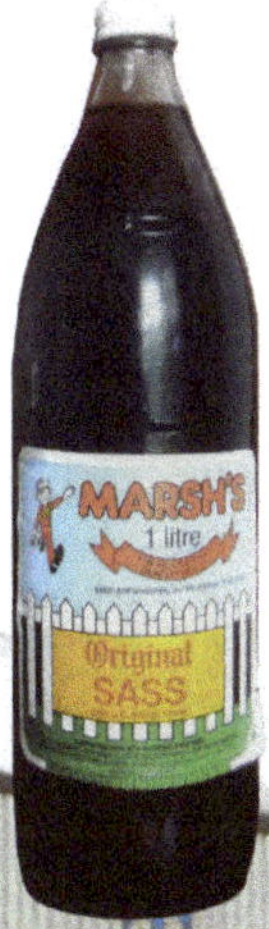

Marsh's Sass in the later style bottle.
It disappeared from shops around 1999.
B.Moxham.

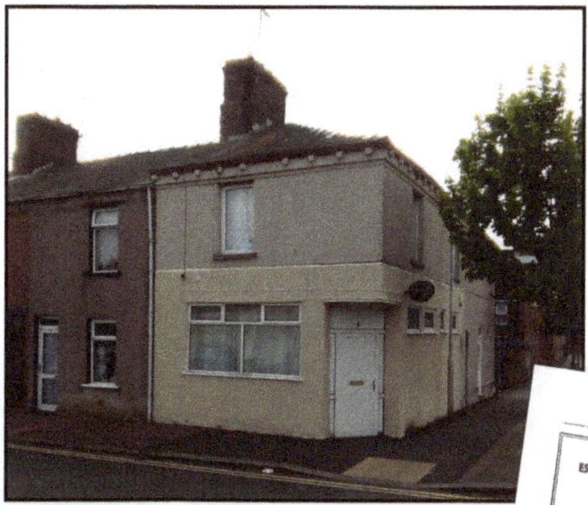

Long before the Tesco Express format had been thought of, the Co-op, at 4 Bath Street, had their own 'express outlet' – Byco, 1957

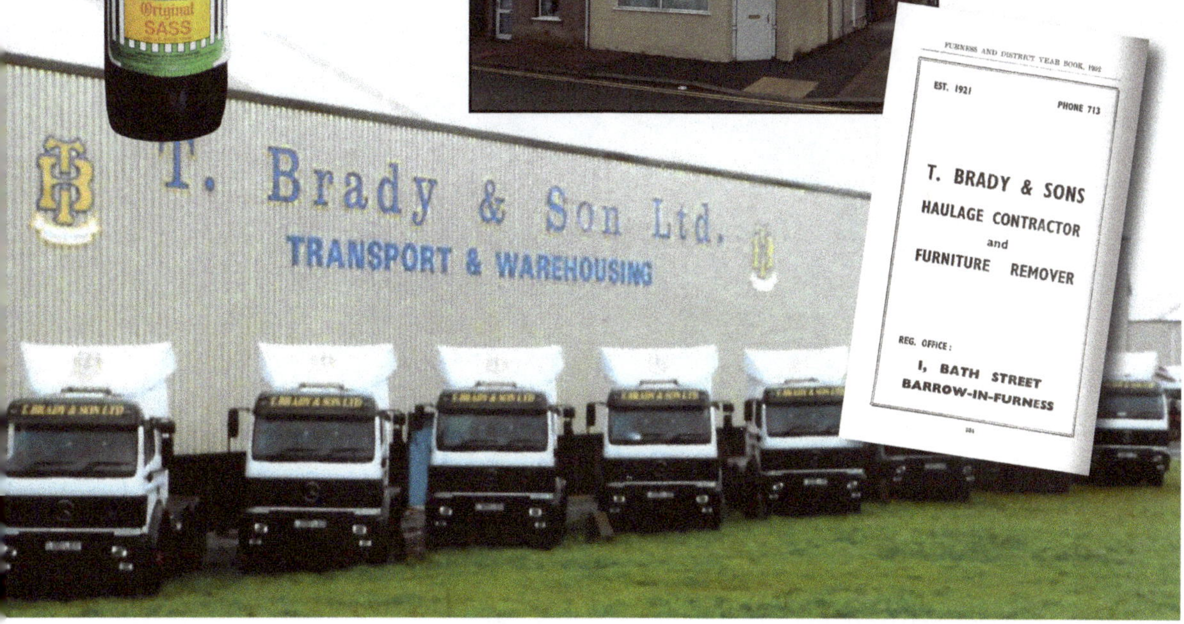

FURNESS AND DISTRICT YEAR BOOK, 1952

EST. 1921

PHONE 713

T. BRADY & SONS

HAULAGE CONTRACTOR

and

FURNITURE REMOVER

REG. OFFICE:

1, BATH STREET

BARROW-IN-FURNESS

Part of the Brady fleet parked on what was originally the Hoop Works site. Courtesy of T. Brady & Son. Brady initially set out, in 1921, with a horse and cart, gradually progressing to tipper lorries; then to 8-wheelers and Artics. Right: Advertisement for Brady's from the Furness and District Yearbook for 1952 Courtesy of Cumbria Local Archives and Study Centre, Barrow.

Bell Family

The Bell Family; Salvage Dealers of Duke Street, L to R are Mr. W J Bell (Manxman); Elizabeth, 2 yrs; Gordon, 3 months; John, aged 5 years. (the Bells were recycling before the term was even coined!) *Bell Family Photo, March 1935*

Appendix Two

Tubal Cain

Offices and Main Entrance of the Hindpool Steel Works

Rules for Accessing the Works

Demolition of a Pioneer Works – Project Furness

Barcon

Re William Killingbeck (Enid Dorr)

Loss of Our Steel Heritage

The Hindpool Ironworks viewed at daybreak across Walney Channel;
This is a reproduction of the original Acrylic on paper, produced for the author by the well-known artist, John Duffin, who was also a work colleague from the Ship Drawing Office of Vickers Ltd.

On the Power of Iron

Old Tubal Cain was a man of might
In the days when the earth was young;
By the fierce red light of his furnace bright
The strokes of his hammer rung;
And he lifted high his brawny hand
On the iron growing clear;
Till the sparks rushed out in scarlet showers
As he fashioned the sword & spear;
And he sang – "Hurrah for my handiwork!
Hurrah for the spear & sword!
Hurrah for the hand that shall wield them well,
For he shall be King and Lord!

Extract from Tubal Cain by Charles Mackay.

Pencil drawing of the General Offices and Main Entrance of the Haematite Steel Company, on Walney Road, depicting the 1930s. *Courtesy of Geoffrey Berry, 2018.*

Believed to have been an early commission for architects Sharpe, Paley and Austin (who would later build the Flax and Jute Works), construction was by William Gradwell and James Garden. Per Local historian, Walter Johnston of the Barrow Civic and Local History Society.

An attempt led by Dr Bill Rollinson, also of the Barrow Civic Society, and supported by a petition raised by local residents to have the edifice preserved, failed. The town council had bowed to pressure and referred the question of preservation to a Lancaster firm for the purpose of feasibility and cost implications. Opinion was that the building could have been scoped into the design of the Furness Business Park. [See also Loss of our Steel Heritage].

"I left Barrow Grammar School during the 1930s and started in the Analytical Laboratory at the steelworks. Coming off-shift I would often see several children, usually bare-foot and probably from the Scotch Buildings, outside of the gate begging for food. Men with leftovers from their bait (lunch) would hand it over to them. This memory has stayed with me". Bill Whiteside, Industrial Chemist.

Regulations for working (using) the entrance to the General Offices.

1st. The front stairs are only to be used by the Directors, General Manager and Secretary.

2nd. Any person wishing to interview the General Manager or Secretary must be shewn up the office stairs, and dealt with by the messengers who will announce them in their turn.

3rd. The whole of the office and Works staff are passed through this entrance.

4th. No person using the workman's entrance and working on check, must, be passed through the office entrance on any pretence whatsoever.

5th. The Staff Attendance book must have a line drawn promptly under the signature of the work's staff at 0-15, 1-15, 1-45 and 2-15.

6th. No tradesmen are admitted to the Works.

7th. Visitors are admitted to the Works as per printed regulation. This rule must be strictly adhered to.

8th. The Commissionaires must on all occasions when the Company's carriages etc., drive up to the offices open the carriage door, salute the occupants and open all doors leading to the General Offices.

9th. The Directors, General Manager and Secretary must be saluted on every occasion in passing through the offices.

10th. The Commissionaire on all occasions when the carriages etc., leave and return to the stables or motor garage, open the entrance doors. The Company's carters open the doors for themselves.

11th. The Commissionaires will when on night duty be required to attend to the stores, and give out what may be required, but on no occasion must stores be given out without an order signed by the head of the department. When any workman is injured on the night turn, the Commissionaire will find all needful appliances in a conspicuous place in the stores, and must attend as well as he can to the wants of the injured.

12th. The Commissionaire on the night turn, will patrol the General Offices every hour after sunset. The time will be kept by a time watch. The slip giving the hours will be sent to the General Manager every morning.

13th. The fire-proof door in the General Offices, near the strong room, must be kept closed at all times.

BY ORDER,

(Signed)   A. J. While*

General Works Manager, B.H.S.Co.

* Augustus While was the son of Director James While. Original document undated but assumed to be between 1910 – 1919, which was the period of his incumbency.

The above regulations illustrate the level of class distinction in existence, between 'blue collar' and office staff, throughout industry during the period. (Transcript from the original document per Cumbria Archives (Barrow), Ref:BD/HJ] Box163]. These rules, by and large, apart from the saluting were still valid during the 1960s - author

Demolition of a Pioneer Works
Project Furness

On the following page is an aerial view of a large proportion of Hindpool taken in the late eighties. It gives a clear picture of just how much land had been occupied by the mighty iron and steelworks for over one hundred years and the scale of Project Furness. Please join me in a circular tour. And so as they say in musical parlance, taking it from the top left-hand corner, we see the Asda Superstore on the site of the Furness Brick and Tile Company, one of the original gate stoops of the Brick Works entrance has been retained. Moving to the right across Asda car park we see the large MFI building (note no Stollers or Matalan yet). We next come to several rows of terraced houses (centre-top of photo), Chatsworth; Melbourne and Adelaide Streets then St James' Junior School with the church just visible at the top. Next is St James' County Infants School and then Blake Street with the Queen's Hotel at the corner of Blake and Duke Streets. Several more rows of houses and then Howard Street Technical College in the top-right corner.

The large expanse of land across the centre of the picture is the cleared Steelworks site with only the offices and main entrance remaining. Demolition of these was deferred pending a discussion as to their fate. [Eleven miles of rail network had once criss-crossed this site; at the time of the photo contractors clearing the site had yet to find a myriad of underground flues and gas culverts].

The Duke of Devonshire's Diary tells us that work on the steel sheds began in March 1865. Hastily constructed despite a scarcity of skilled labour but in true Victorian fashion, time was found to adorn the top of the bell housing atop No.2 shed with a fleur-de-lis. *Photo 02/08/78 by K. E. Royall.*

Prior to the works being established this had been agricultural land comprising of the fields – Near Hazelgill; Middle Hazelgill; Near Millbank; West Millbank and Far Meadow.

Across the fore-ground we see the engineering facility that once serviced the Hindpool bf plant, later Barrow Ironworks Ltd. At the time of the photo it was being operated by the Barrow Engineering Company and it employed around 60 people. Their offices can be seen in the lower-right quadrant of the photo (a single story building with five vehicles parked outside). Managing Director was James McWhan who had previously been the commercial manager of Barrow Ironworks. Walney Channel can be seen along the bottom of the frame.

The Hindpool industrial site almost cleared – Project Furness, c. 1990
Aerial photo courtesy of T. Brady and Son.

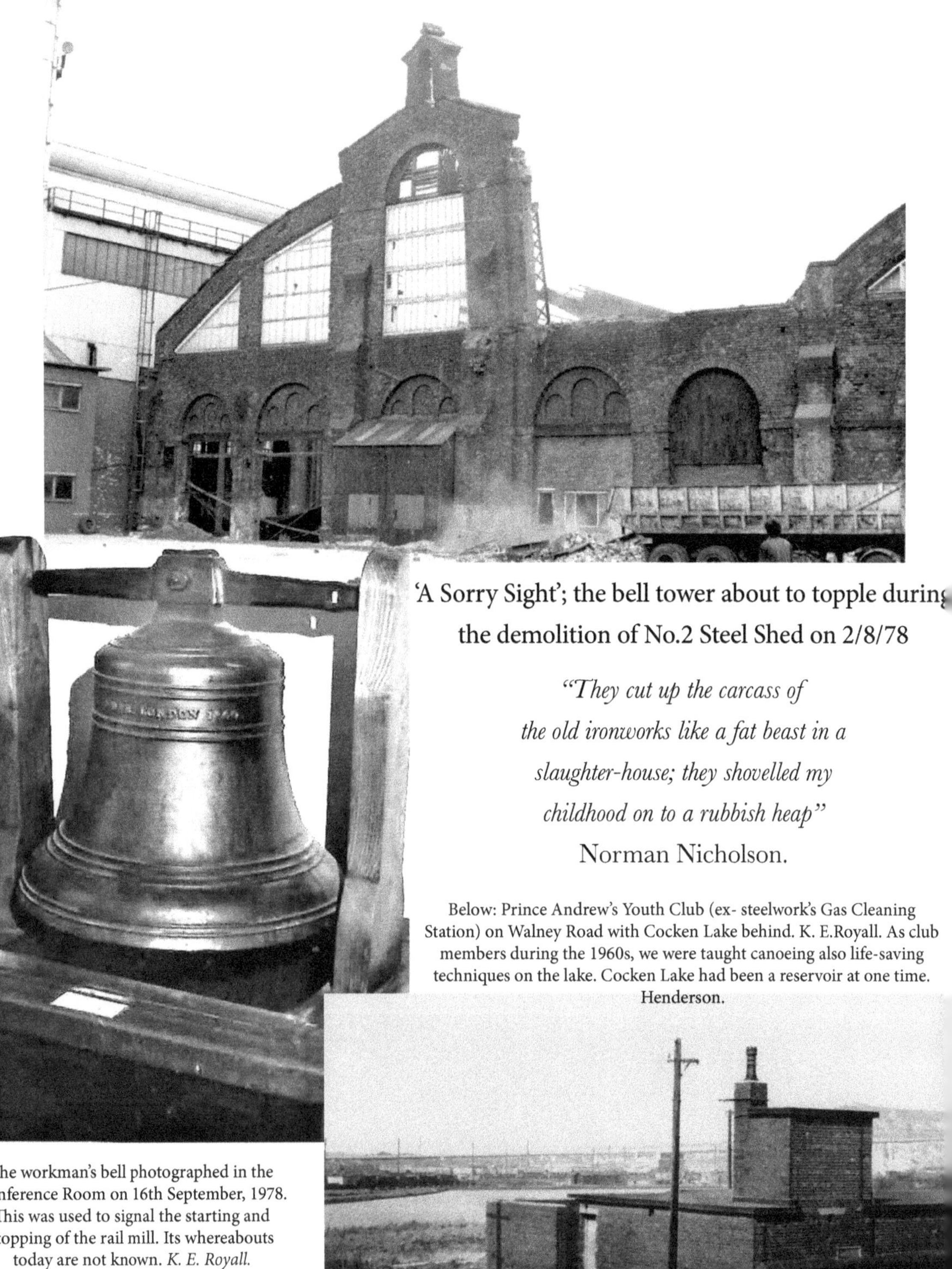

'A Sorry Sight'; the bell tower about to topple during the demolition of No.2 Steel Shed on 2/8/78

"They cut up the carcass of the old ironworks like a fat beast in a slaughter-house; they shovelled my childhood on to a rubbish heap" Norman Nicholson.

Below: Prince Andrew's Youth Club (ex- steelwork's Gas Cleaning Station) on Walney Road with Cocken Lake behind. K. E.Royall. As club members during the 1960s, we were taught canoeing also life-saving techniques on the lake. Cocken Lake had been a reservoir at one time. Henderson.

The workman's bell photographed in the Conference Room on 16th September, 1978. This was used to signal the starting and stopping of the rail mill. Its whereabouts today are not known. *K. E. Royall.*

Interior of the derelict Gas Engine House photographed in the mid-1990s by visiting architect Tim Russell. Shortly after this was taken, the building was rased. *Photo Tim Russell courtesy of R. Bradley.*

The Gas Engine House shortly after it was commissioned in 1909, it housed six in number 1850-bhp double acting, single-crank engines driving generators and blowers for the bf plant. It had been reported in the Trade Press that it was the largest engine house in the World. It qualified as such, apparently, in that it had no supporting internal structures i.e. pillars or bulkheads, per Bill Pearson, ex-works.

BARCON

This 1961 photo shows the new continuous casting machines just prior to being commissioned. At the time they were the 'last word' in steelmaking technology. The high-speed Barrow process was developed at Hindpool and visited by delegates from works as far away as Japan. During the early 1960s it was regularly visited by groups of schoolchildren. I was lucky to have had my own, personal, guided tour – and it blew me away! (Upon entering the works for the first few times I had felt strong bodily reactions, mainly in my chest and neck, consistent with my first visit to York Minster. Was this just a reaction to grandeur, or was it something more profoundly fundamental?). *Photo courtesy of K.Royall.*

William Killingbeck

(Ref Chap. 3)

From the end of the war and up to his death in 1959, Mr Killingbeck's personal secretary had been Kathleen Enid Allington, nee Dorr. Known as Enid, she started with the Company in 1937 where she joined the staff of the Correspondence Office but quickly aspiring to secretarial status. She was a remarkable woman in that she attained Pitman shorthand of 140-wpm with Distinction. Enid was also holder of a Pitman Diploma for teaching shorthand.

In the works she joined the private in-house Air Raid Precautions Scheme, qualified in St John's First Aid and also the work's Anti Gas Training. She also played piano. Enid lived with her husband Vic (they had no children), at 1, Flass Lane, Barrow and then at Ridding Bay, Lakeside, Newby Bridge. This had previously been a guest house and had been bought by her parents in 1945. At the top of the stairs at Ridding Bay was one of the original Andrew's paintings of the works. Enid was truly representative of the calibre of person responsible for making the works at Barrow World famous. She died in 2004 in Furness General Hospital.

Enid at work in 1940 next to an early type of (hand-operated) copier.

Enid (standing), pictured at her home at Ridding Bay, with friends c. 1980
Courtesy of B. Cubbon.

MANY MOURN DEATH OF MR. KILLINGBECK

Minister's tribute at funeral service

THE Mayor and Mayoress of Barrow, Coun. and Mrs. M. Bolt, and representatives of industry in the North-west were among those who attended the funeral today of Mr. William Killingbeck, chairman and managing director of Barrow Ironworks, who died suddenly in London on Wednesday.

The service, at Barrow Emmanual Congregational Church, was conduted by the minister, the Rev. V. Leach. Mrs. E. Sharpe was the organist.

The service was followed by private cremation at Blackpool.

Mr. Leach said of Mr. Killingbeck: "He was loved not only for himself but for his works sake.

"He revelled not only in his work but also in the many activities for the good of the community for which he laboured. Everything that he did, he did it with characteristic energy and drive, and that meant that he did much more than many others could have done.

'A GRIEVOUS BURDEN'

"His sudden passing from us brings a grievous burden to those he loved and to us all, a burden that is all the heavier because it has been thrust upon us without warning. But he would not have been happy if he had lived to be unable to do and to work. He died with his flag flying.

"His service to local industry was very considerable and he worked magnimously. Although he pursued his work with energy and zeal it was never at the expense of those who worked under him. He was always considerate and kindly towards others and never riding roughshod over the feelings of others."

'FAMILY MAN'

Mr. Leach said the loss felt by people of Barrow was nothing compared with the loss felt in Mr. Killingbeck's home. "He was a family man, indeed, and nothing pleased him more than to be at home with his wife, family and grandchildren."

The flowers in the church were from his family and Barrow Ironworks.

The family mourners were: Mrs. W. Killingbeck (widow), Mr. and Mrs. Barry Charles (son-in-law and daughter), Miss Mary Killingbeck (daughter).

OTHER MOURNERS

Other mourners were:
Mr. S. S. Wilson (secretary of and representing the Iron and Steel Holding and Realisation Agency), Sir John Fisher (governing director of James Fisher and Sons, Ltd., and director of Barrow Ironworks Ltd.), Lady Fisher, Mr. R. B. Sharp (assistant managing director Barrow Ironworks Ltd.), Mrs. Sharp, Mr. J. Williamson (director and secretary, Barrow Ironworks Ltd.)

Mr. T. G. Marple (general manager, Barrow Steelworks Ltd), Mrs. Marple, Mr. J. A. Clark (manager, representing Barrow Haematite Steel Co., Ltd., and Barrow Quarries, Ltd.), Mrs. Clark, Mr. H. C. Gill (representing Messrs. Parkinson, Mather and Co., Manchester), Mr. F. B. Hart Jackson (Messrs. Hart Jackson and Sons, Ulverston), Mrs. Hart Jackson.

Mrs. W. J. Elliott (representing Messrs. Peat, Marwick, Mitchell and Co.), Mr. A. Storey (director and general manager, Vickers Armstrongs Engineers Ltd., also representing Mr. W. D. Opher, managing director Vickers - Armstrongs Engineers Ltd., and a director of the Shipbuilding Co., and Mrs. Opher), Mr. L. Redshaw (director and shipbuilding general manager, Vickers-Armstrongs Shipbuilders Ltd.), Mrs. Redshaw, Mr. S. M. Gardner (Vickers - Armstrongs Engineers Ltd., also representing Mr. and Mrs. E. P. Laurens and family) Mr. T. S. Durham (representing Lord Lonsdale), Mr. E. A. Slater (representing the Duke of Buccleuch).

Mr. T. S. Kilpatrick (director and general manager, Workington Iron and Steel Co.), Mr. T. Crosier (Messrs. David Caird Ltd.), Mr. V. H. Crozier (Vickers-Armstrongs Engineers Ltd.), Mr. J. Scott (representing Millom Haematite Ore and Iron Co., the Pig Iron Producers' Conference and the National Association of Haematite Pig Iron Makers), Mr. W. E. Grainger (acting divisional traffic manager, British Railways, Barrow), Mr. A. P. Grieve (assistant district traffic superintendent, Commercial, also representing Mr. A. Higginson, district traffic superintendent, British Railways, London Midland Region).

Mr. B. Winder (director Vickers-Armstrongs (Engineers) Ltd.), Mrs. Winder, Mr. Lawrence Allen (Town Clerk, Barrow), Mr. D. A. Savage (manager, Ministry of Labour, Barrow) Mr. H. W. Hargreaves (manager, District Bank Ltd., Barrow), Mr. L. Larkinson (Lloyds Bank Ltd. Barrow), Mr. A. A. I. Walker (Barclays Bank Ltd.), Mr. K. D'Alby (docks manager, Barrow, also representing Sir Robert Letch, British Transport Docks).

County Coun. W. D. Coope (representing Lancashire County Council), Supt. E. J. Williamson (Deputy Chief Constable, Barrow representing Mr. S. Ballance, Chief Constable and Barrow Police Force), Mr. T. Colquhoun (United Steel Companies), Ald. G. D. Hastwell, Mr. S. J. Fisher (representing North Lonsdale Agricultural Society).

Mr. Alan Milligan (Lakeland Laundries Ltd.), Mr. J. H. Peck (Thos. W. Ward Ltd., Sheffield), Mr. M. N. Fleming (Thos. W. Ward Ltd., Barrow) Mr. P. Williams (Thos. W. Ward Ltd., Sheffield), Mr. R. B. Davies (Hodbarrow Mines, Millom).

Miss P. James (matron, North Lonsdale Hospital), Mr. J. Connell (Barrow Sailors' Home), Mr. W. W. Randall (representing Randall and Porter, Ulverston); Mr. R. C. Ashcroft (Walmsley and Smith), Mr. J. J. Darby (chief accountant, Barrow Ironworks, Ltd.); Mr. J. C. Kay (manager, Pennington Ore Mill); Mr. W. G. Welch (James Fisher and Sons, Ltd.).

Mr. A. Tilburn, Mr. E. Hannaway, Miss Eleanor Heys, Mr. A. Allington, Mr. A. A. Atkinson, Mr. A. W. McLaren, Mrs. C. Kite, Mrs. E. Armistead, Mr. W. G. Wilson, Mr. C. Bland, Mr. A. F. West, Mr. J. H. Eason.

Mrs. S. Douglas, Mr. C. Allen, Mr. W. Alcey, Mr. G. A. Leech, Mr. S. Sirett, Mr. H. Careless, Mr. W. Coward, Mr. C. Faulkner, Mr. Butcher, Mr. E. Thompson, Mr. J. Atkinson, Mr. H. Atkinson.

Mr. J. E. Smith, Mr. F. Hudson, Mr. G. Newton, Mr. A. J. M. Mason, Mrs. A. Logan, Mr. P. M. Rainey, Mr. F. G. Thompson, Mr. W. B. Longstaff, Dr. Bruce Mayne, Mr. and Mrs. W. Park, Miss B. Bayne.

Mr. J. Green, Mr. and Mrs. N. Coyle, Mr. G. T. Kinrade, Mr. W. H. Jones, Mr. J. Whalley, Mr. G. Johnson, Dr. T. H. Forsythe, Mr. W. Horner, Mr. G. C. Croasdale, Miss S. Gardner, Miss J. York, Dr. A. Rankin.

Dr. R. Forbes-Jones, Mr. J. M. Dixon, Mr. W. M. Bowles, Dr. G. H. Harvey, Mr. J. K. Howarth, Mr. G. H. Rowe, Mr. and Mrs. R. B. Sharp, Mr. W. Collinge, Mr. and Mrs. N. Noble, Mr. W. J. Daley, Mr. J. Milner.

Mr. Cornett, Mr. T. R. Hesketh, Mr. A. Hindmarch, Mr. W. C. Fairbairn (chairman, Westmorland branch of the St. George Society) Mr. T. E. Pollock (St. Andrews Society), Mr. W. Eccles (St. Andrews Society), Mr. D. Steel (St. Andrews Society).

Mr. W. Steel (representing Barrow Ironworks Ambulance Corps), Mr. J. E. Cummings, Mr. E. Walker (representing Stainton Quarry Ambulance Corps), Mr. W. Jackson (Barrow Ambulance League), Mr. J. Holgate (chairman of Barrow Centre St. John Ambulance Association), Mr. R. Hutchinson (Barrow Centre, St. John Ambulance Association).

Mr. J. E. Baker and Mr. J. Dall (Barrow A.F.C.), Mrs. Dall, Mr. H. Reid, Mr. E. Sandham, Mr. S. J. Morrison, Mr. and Mrs. Ryan, Mr. M. E. Pullard, Mr. and Mrs. Robert Airey, Mrs. M. H. Wood, Mr. J. E. Thompson, Mr. H. Atkinson, Mr. and Mrs. W. I. Towers.

Mr. P. J. Williams, Mrs. J. Milner, Mr. and Mrs. R. Darbyshire, Mr. S. Green, Mr. R. H. Young, Mr. E. J. Langtree, Mr. A. D. Langtree, Dr. and Mrs. W. J. Liddle, Mrs. J. Maltby Black, Mrs. J. B. Jackson, Mr. K. W. Bishop, Mr. S. Jackson, Mr. K. W. Jacques.

Mr. W. Case, Mr. A. Norris, Mr. W. Coward Mr. G. A. Westwood, Mr. A. W. Maxton, Mrs. B. Leach, Mr. E. Hatton, Mr. F. F. Horne, Mr. H. Holmes, Mr. B. Williams, Col. J. R. S. Thompson, Mr. D. Saul, Mrs. Pass, Mr. and Mrs. E. Sankey, Mr. A. Chill, Mr. S. Holme, Mr. J. W. Dickinson, Mr. A. Paterson, Mr. C. Fitzsimmons, Mr. H. Gardner, Mr. H. Garner, Jun., Coun. T. McNulty, Mr. J. Lyon, Mr. W. Bryant, Mr. J. Sandiford, Mr. A. W. Warbrick, Dr. Wilson Miller, Mr. A. R. Millard, Mr. J. Hardisty, Mr. and Mrs. N. Spencer, Mrs. W. Flowerday, Mrs. L. Egerton, Mrs. M. Elliott, Mr. H. C. Gill, Mr. and Mrs. T. Banks, Mr. F. L. Gilbert, Mr. S. A. Gilbert Mr. E. Atkinson, Mr. R. W. Wilkinson, Mr. James Arnott, Mr. John Sutton, Mr. G. C. Harrison, Mr. and Mrs. R. Worton, Mr. James Ellis, Mr. G. Mccalfe, Mr. E. G. Kite, Mr. H. Kenyon.

★ See Page Ten

The Loss of our Steel Heritage

An unfortunate milestone in the history of the Barrow works was becoming just an annex of Workington steelworks during the 1970s. Barrow, which could make any type and grade of steel, became subordinate to a works with no steelmaking capability, (Workington's Bessemer plant had shut down in 1974). It would become clear that Barrow was placed under Workington to facilitate a run down and then closure. British Steel appointed Max De Redder from Gilcrux, Cumbria, as closure manager. Over a period of around 3-years, De Redder began systematically transferring 'items' from Hindpool to Workington. This activity became a cause of concern for some union representatives at Barrow. Jim McGlennon, works convenor, made representations to local management about what he perceived as being tantamount to 'looting'. His protestations fell upon deaf ears (Jim's original hand-written letter about the matter now resides with Cumbria Archives and Local Studies Centre, Barrow).

Between us it was agreed that I would write direct to Mr De Redder requesting

BARROW steelworks union stalwart Jim McGlennon has been presented with a Confederation Shield, eight months after being made redundant.

The Confederation Shield was presented to Jim on behalf of the Executive Council by Eric Caudwell (left) who paid tribute to Jim's sterling qualities.

Jim replied that it had always been a great pleasure to do what he could for the union and for his fellow workers. He had found particularly challenging the union activity in the last six of his 34 years' employment at the steel works.

Photo: Nick Lockett of the North-Western Evening Mail.

Jim McGlennon receiving his award for services to the Union. Photo: 1982.
Jim was a furnaceman on No 3 Hoop Mill; he lived on Anson Street in Hindpool.
Courtesy of I.S.K.T. Banner

a copy of his inventory. (My own enquiries established that, outside of working for British Steel, the man was an antiques collector with, also, a passion for vintage motor cars). In a nutshell, I was told that the items belonged to British Steel and that it was really none of my business. The 'items' in question, which comprised of Victoriana, such as office furniture and equipment – time pieces – original paintings and 19th century equipment from the Test House. These items, to us, were a part of the town's steelmaking heritage and belonged in the museum here. All that my efforts achieved was to be sent a Polaroid snap of a workman rolling a cigarette, apparently the winner of the hoop work's cigarette hand-rolling competition. I had been fobbed-off.

About ten years later, by which time De Redder had passed away, I wrote to his widow. In her reply she denied the existence of an inventory, telling me that any items from Barrow had been placed in The Lodge, a British Steel guest house on the outskirts of Workington and that I should be happy that the Barrow things were still in the County. My next step was to address an open letter to ex-British Steel personnel via the Cumberland Times & Star. Whilst this did elicit several responses, nothing concrete emerged. Then, with the subsequent closure of the works at Moss Bay in 2004, our heritage became lost for all time. We will never know precisely what left the town.

Is this one of the reasons why very little exists in Barrow's Dock Museum, regarding our steelmaking past?

With acknowledgements to ex-school friend, Charles Hamilton, for information pertaining to Mr. De Redder.

Left: A view from the northern-end of the steelworks looking towards Upper Hindpool; the end of Bath Street, almost at its junction with Walney Road, can be seen. Looking over the roof of Brisbane Park Infants School we see the terrace of larger houses on Blake Street and then the Town Hall with the spire of St Mary of Furness to the right. *Courtesy of Brian Moxham.*

Believed to have been the longest slag heap in Europe. It comprised upwards of 9-million tons of slag – the by-product of the Hindpool blast furnaces. It has however now been reduced, reshaped, turfed and planted. Referred to by some as Barrow's Mountain, it incorporates a foot-path with impressive views across to Walney Island and beyond. It is the only tangible remains of the works on the original site and stands yet to remind us of a once proud industry. *Photo Graham Kidd.*

Also by the same author

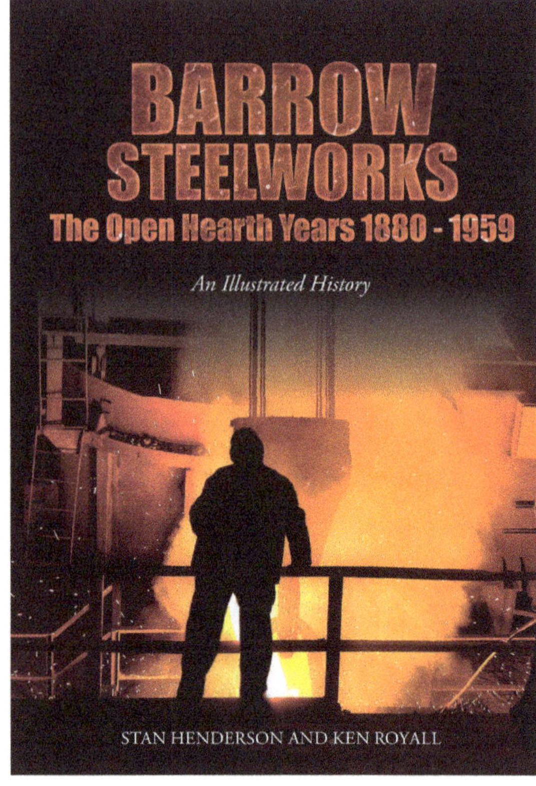

During the second half of the nineteenth century, Barrow-in-Furness became a pioneer in iron and steel production. It went on to grow astronomically – owning collieries in three counties and ore mines in two – and became the largest integrated steelworks in north Lancashire and Cumberland and, at one time, the largest steelworks in the world. Its success was due, in part, to having the prestige of three dukes as directors, as well as to being only 2 miles away from one of the largest and richest iron ore mines in the country.

The 1880s were a decade of change for Barrow works with some of the main players departing the scene. The arrival of the basic method of steelmaking, took away the lucrative position held by the directors and shareholders who had drained the coffers leaving virtually nothing for re-investment. After the Great War the company was limping along. The evacuation of Dunkirk at the start of WWII together with the blocking of special steels produced a demand for the kind of steel the making of which Barrow was a past master. Under United Steel's banner Barrow would see security of employment.

Paperback: 160 pages Publisher: The History Press; Language: English ISBN-13: 978-0750963787	

| Paperback: 98 pages
Publisher: Stanley Henderson
Language: English
ISBN-13: 978-0995619050 | available at amazon |

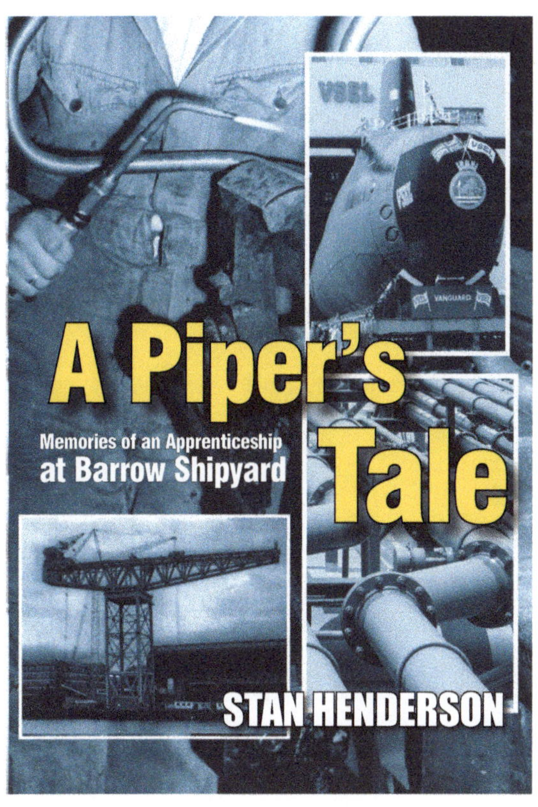

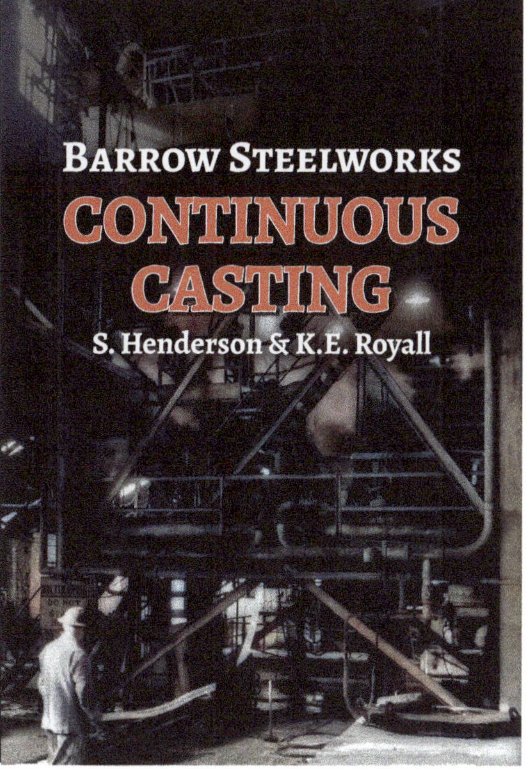

A Pipers Tale records the impressions made on a teenager as he makes his way into the thorny world of shipbuilding. A world in which the author, during the 1960s, witnessed the change from traditional shipbuilding, where vessels were constructed with a minimum, but adequate, level of technical support via long established trade practices and skills, to the cutting-edge of science-based projects as the Yard at Barrow became a 'Leader in Marine Technology' with the making of sophisticated warships and first-of-class vessels. Saluting the the wealth of characters and personalities that comprised the Yard's Plumbing Fraternity.

Since the end of the Second World War (1939-1945), there have been some outstanding technical developments in steelmaking, which have since been adopted on a worldwide basis. These developments include the use of oxygen in bulk; automation; high-speed rolling and continuous casting. During the 50s & 60s, the works at Barrow adopted all four initiatives in varying degrees. Most notable for us was the development of High-Speed Continuous Casting. In this book the authors are attempting to lay down a permanent record of what was achieved locally and thereby, hopefully, preserving the memory of a once-proud industry.

Paperback: 96 pages
Publisher: Stanley Henderson
Language: English
ISBN-13: 978-0995619081

available at

Paperback: 88 pages
Publisher: Stanley Henderson
Language: English
ISBN-13: 978-1913898243

available at
amazon

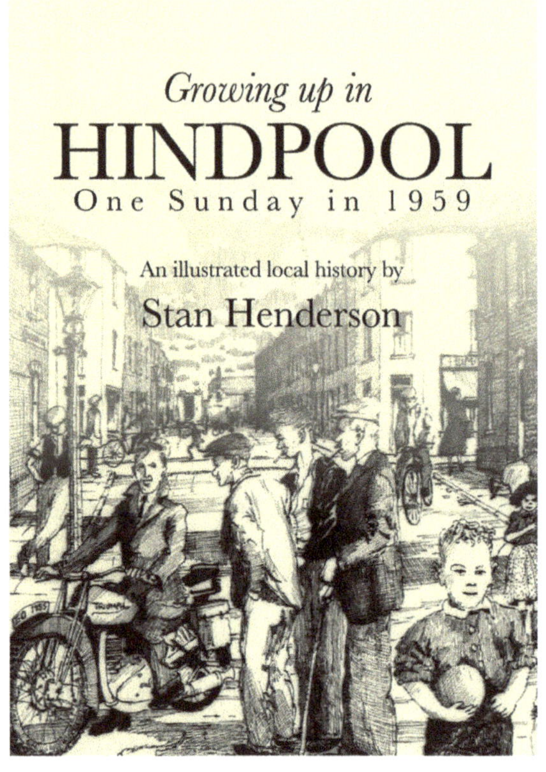

Morecambe Back in My Day is the story of a childhood idyll, which is still strongly evocative. It is a memoir based on experiences spent in a resort referred to by the Victorians as 'Naples of The North'.

The author has pieced together a tapestry of fun times and memorable occasions using information and images from family records. It has been written about with affection and sincerity.

In this follow-up to Growing Up in Hindpool, the author completes his patchwork quilt with respect to the industries, institutions and businesses to which he has been directly or indirectly involved. The reader is taken on a walk out of the district and, via Lower Cocken, into Ormsgill, then back into Hindpool. During this walk, which 60-years ago, was undertaken at least once per week, the author reflects upon aspects of 1950's life, bygone industries, landmarks and some of the local characters that made Hindpool one of Barrow's most fascinating places in which to belong.

Paperback: 72 pages
Publisher: Stanley Henderson
Language: English
ISBN-13: 978-1913898823

Paperback: 84 pages
Publisher: Stanley Henderson
Language: English
ISBN-13: 978-1916275836

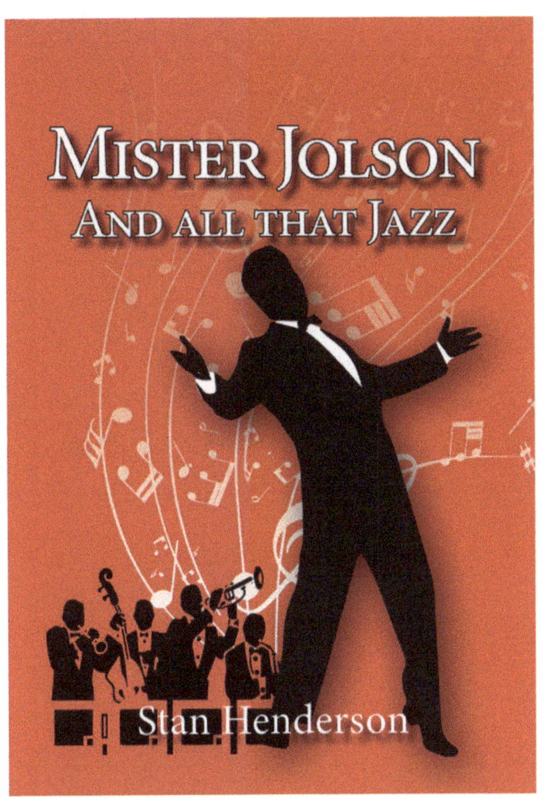

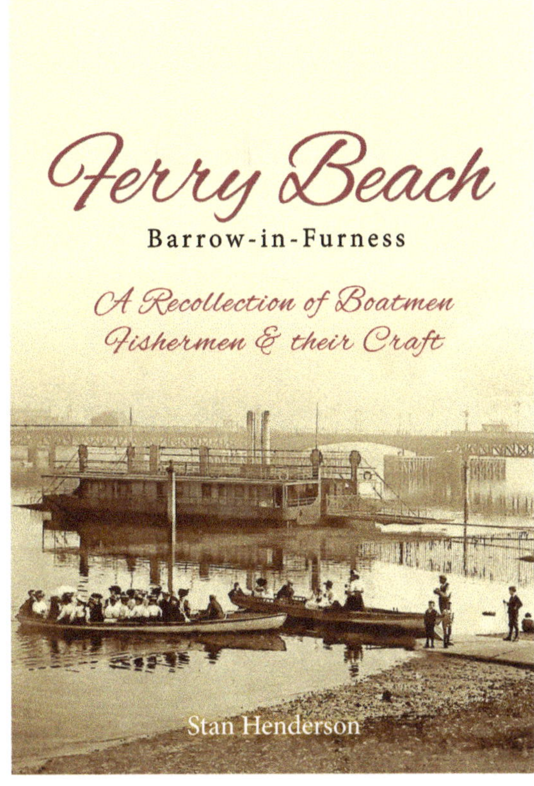

In this book, which is an appreciation of the popular art, the author takes us on a fleeting excursion through the evolution of 'pop' - from ragtime to hot jazz and in to the swing era - a fascinating insight into the early Broadway Musical and the birth of the 'talkies'.

The emergence of the Great American Song Book, and the influence of Al Jolson's career on popular singing; his relationship with the principal song writers, and how he inspired the great vocal stars who followed, including Ethel Waters, Bing Crosby, Judy Garland and Frank Sinatra.

Ferry Beach is a captivating recollection of the men and boats that have sailed the waters around Barrow-in-Furness for generations. Through personal anecdotes and historical research, author Stan Henderson paints a vivid portrait of the boatmen who braved the waves, wind, and tides to make their living on the sea. Ferry Beach explores the many types of craft that have graced the waters off Barrow and is a tribute to the people who crewed them - the hardworking, skilled, and often colourful characters who kept the maritime traditions of the region alive. It offers a glimpse into a world that has largely disappeared.

<table>
<tr><td>Paperback: 92 pages
Publisher: Stanley Henderson
Language: English
ISBN-13: 978-1913898045</td><td>
</td></tr>
</table>

<table>
<tr><td>Paperback: 72 pages
Publisher: Stanley Henderson
Language: English
ISBN-13: 978-1913898731</td><td>
</td></tr>
</table>